Monaco, Monte Carlo Information Tourism

Travel Guide, Early History, Economy, Culture and Tradition

Author
Bobby Chapman.

Publisher:
SONITTEC LTD
College House, 2nd Floor
17 King Edwards Road,
Ruislip
London
HA4 7AE

Table of Content

Summary

Travel around the world we live in?
1. (Traveling is easier than you think): We believe that traveling around the world shouldn't be hard: it's actually something everyone should be able to do at least once in their lives. Whether you choose to spend a few years or just a couple months traveling this beautiful planet, it's important to see what's out there. It's up to you to make the dream come true and take the first step. Launch Trip Planner to piece together and price your ideal route. Not sure where to start? You can always call one of our travel consultants and get some complimentary advice!

2.(Travel opens your eyes).: If you're open and willing, travel will make you an incredibly more well-rounded human being. And that's really the goal, isn't it? If you don't know where to start, check out our Around the World planning guide.

3. (Traveling helps you learn who you are).: All the challenges and opportunities travel lays at your feet help you discover who you are in a way that's only possible on the road.

4. (Travel creates meaningful relationships): People you meet while on the road become some of the most valued names on your contact list. They become places on the map to visit later on. These folks give you a glimpse outside your hometown circle of friends, and force you to take in new and refreshing perspectives, and ultimately realize that everyone is the same.

5. (Traveling develops skills you didn't know you had): Sometimes it's only far from home that you realize you you've got skills you've never used. It's travel that brings them to the surface and makes you smile, satisfied to have reached the mountain top, or crossed a gorge or helped a villager clean up after a storm, or even to have successfully ordered a meal at a rural Chinese restaurant.

6. (Travel helps you learn new languages): There's something satisfying about being able to throw around a few words of Greek, knowing how to say thanks in Thai, pulling out that long dormant Spanish to book a room in Santiago, or simply hearing a language you didn't know existed just a few weeks before.

7. (Travel means adventure): Zip-lining over the jungle canopy in Peru, successfully navigating the maze-like streets of Venice, bartering for the best

price in the traditional markets of Marrakech, taking a speedboat ride in New Zealand, or hopping in a Land Rover and heading out to watch animals grazing in Tanzania: these are adventures worth having. People are hardwired for the excitement of adventure and travel may just be the best way to tap into it.

8. (Traveling gives you perspective): Meeting people from other cultures will teach you that the way you've been looking at the world isn't the way everybody else does. In fact, your point-of-view might have some major blind spots. Seeing the world for yourself will improve your vision and your grip on reality.

9. (Travel helps you move forward): If you're between jobs, schools, kids, or relationships, around the world travel can be a perfect way to move from one of these life stages into your next

great adventure. A big trip won't just ease your transition into the next stage of your life, it'll give you a chance to reflect on where you've been, where you're going, and where you want to end up.

10. (Travel is education): Seeing the world provides an education that's absolutely impossible get in school. Travel teaches you economy, politics, history, geography, and sociology in an intense, hands-on way no class will. Fortunately, the school of travel is always taking applications, no entrance exam required.

11. (Travel challenges you): Getting your daily latte at the same place and staring at your screen at your nine-to-five every day not nearly interesting enough? Even if you choose to work on the road (and keep staring at the screen), you'll have to find a new place to drink your latte, and depending on

your destination, finding coffee, and foamy milk or a good place to sip them could prove to be a sizeable challenge. Travel is full of moments of joy and challenges. Overcoming the challenges gives you some of the greatest joys of all.

12. (Travel shakes things up): It sucks to be stuck in a rut. Everyone knows what that's like. A big trip can be your perfect solution. Fly around the world, stopping over in all of the places you've always wanted to visit. Go ahead and plan your ideal route around the world (it's easier than you think!)

13. (Traveling proves that dreams do come true): You imagined it, daydreamed about it, envisioned it. Guess what? It can be done. Around the world travel is possible, you just have to decide you're willing to take the first step and start planning your itinerary. What are you waiting for? We've put

together some specials to inspire you to live your dream.

14. (Travel gives you cool stories): Let's face it. Even for folks who can't tell a story, just the words "last year in Mongolia" get you instant party points. Even when events seem trivial, nostalgia and distance create an irresistible spin that makes mundane things like getting your laundry done in Zanzibar, entertaining. Just don't be that person and overdo it!

15. (Travel is literally food for thought).: You'll be constantly surprised at the flavors the world has to offer. The way people in other cultures and countries prepare food, and break bread together (not that all cultures even eat bread) will astound you.

16. (Travel gives you a sense of accomplishment): If you're the kind of person that dreams big, you're

probably one to reach for new challenges. Finishing a trip gives you the satisfaction that you were able make a goal to travel and accomplish what you set out to do see the world.

17. (Traveling for the hell of it): Why travel? Because you can. Because you want to. Because it beats the alternative (staying home). Why not pick up your tickets and get the ball rolling!

Introduction

Monaco is without doubt the most luxurious and glamorous vacation destination in the Mediterranean. Attracting both royalty and the rich and famous, the beaches and marinas are packed with visitors every summer. A principality ruled by Prince Albert II, Monaco has had a long connection to the movie industry. The Prince's late mother was American actress Grace Kelly and the country has widely been featured in blockbusters such as James Bond's *Golden Eye*, *Iron Man 2* and *Ocean's 12*.

Monaco is the second smallest nation in the world, after the Vatican. It's located in the south of

France, and many visitors arriving by car may not even notice they've entered a new territory. With a population of just under 40,000, the locals are known as Monegasques, but only make up about 20 percent of the total population. Residents in the peak summer months can easily double or triple, especially when adding visitors from the numerous Mediterranean cruise ships that dock in Monaco.

The Grimaldi family which has ruled Monaco for over 700 years has brought prosperity and glamour to the country. They have actively promoted the arts, which has led Monaco to host some of the most prestigious events and festivals in the world. Top billings include the Monaco Grand Prix, the annual fireworks display and the Monaco Yacht Show. Also known for its fabulous Monte Carlo casino, the gaming arena epitomizes opulence and wealth.

Summer is the most popular and expensive time to visit Monaco, but this does not deter their typical visitors. It is possible to find deals in the off-season, particularly in the spring and winter. Ultimately however, the majority of visitors to Monaco are day-trippers from nearby towns on the Cote d'Azur. Monaco is home to some of the top restaurants in Europe, many with Michelin stars and long waiting lists that require advance reservations.

Monaco does not have its own airport, which means the bulk of visitors come by car or ship. The closest air hub is Nice Cote d'Azur Airport in France, a half hour drive. The principality's main dock, Port Hercules, attracts Mediterranean cruise ships on a daily basis during the peak summer months. Monaco is well-connected to the French rail network, providing excellent direct rides to major cities in France and Italy.

Monaco is easy to reach by the French motorway and is just a short drive from the Italian border, as well. Roads into Monaco are scenic, yet curvy so be careful navigating the coastal drive. Once inside, it is easy to explore the city on foot, as walking from one end to the other only takes 45 minutes!

History

Monaco: Quaternary Era to 1215

Since the very early days, since the Quaternary Era and perhaps even before, the Rock of Monaco has provided a refuge for primitive peoples, traces of whom have been found in a cave in Saint Martin's Gardens.

The Ligurians

The first inhabitants of our area, the Ligurians, probably arrived when the immigrant warriors who spoke an Indo-European language first penetrated into Provence and Liguria. Ancient authors, the historian Diodorus Siculus and the geographer Strabon, described the Ligurians as a race of mountaineers used to the hardest work and practicing an exemplary frugality.

The Legend of Heracles (Hercules) and the name of "Monaco"

The opening of the route which runs parallel to the coast from Italy to Spain, together with the construction of the old fortifications which were found there, were attributed by the peoples of the past to the great hero of Greek mythology, Heracles, known to the Romans as Hercules. Altars were dedicated to him at the main crossroads of the modest road known as "The Road of Hercules". A complete temple was consecrated to him in the Ligurian port of Monaco. Throughout antiquity, this place was known as Port Hercules. Phoecian and Carthagenian sailors contributed to its prosperity.

The name "Monaco", "Monoikos" in Greek, is nearly always associated with that of Hercules by the ancient writers.

In Greek, Heracles Monoikos may mean "Heracles alone" or "Heracles who has only one temple". This is popular etymology. The name "Monoikos" is certainly a native one and must have its origin in the Ligurian language. It does not appear to be the name of a tribe. The coast and the harbor of Monaco were probably the outlet to the sea for a great Ligurian people of the hinterland, the Oratelli of Peille.

While the Roman period lasted, Monaco was part of the Province of the Maritime Alps. Julius Caesar embarked from its harbor on his way to lead his campaign in Greece. After the fall of the Roman Empire in the fifth century, the whole region was ravaged by the barbarians; this period of invasions lasted until the end of the tenth century. After the expulsion of the Saracens in 975, little by little people began to return to live on the Ligurian coast.

Monaco: 1215 To 1662

The history of Monaco is only known in detail from the thirteenth century. The date of June 10, 1215 marks the birth of the future Principality: on that day, the Genoese Ghibellines led by Fulco del Cassello, who had long since seen the strategic importance of the Rock and was aware of the advantages of the harbor, came there to lay the first stone of the fortress, on whose foundations the Prince's Palace lies today. They had previously obtained from the Emperor Henry VI, the successor of Frederick Barbarossa, sovereignty over the whole country and had acquired the land necessary to carry out their project. The fortress was re-inforced by ramparts, which gradually formed a complete girdle right round the Rock. In order to attract residents, they granted new arrivals valuable privileges such as concessions of land and exemptions from taxes. Monaco thus became, in spite of the small area of its territory, an important place whose possession was to become the subject, during the three centuries which followed, of continual strife, capture and recapture by the representatives of the two parties, the Guelphs and the Ghibellines. The Rock of Monaco was in turn in the hands of the Ghibellines, the Dorias and the Spinolas, supporters of the Emperor and the Guelphs, the Fieschis and the Grimaldis, adherents of the Pope.

Among the families of the Genoese aristocracy belonging to the Guelph party, one of the most brilliant was the Grimaldi family; its most anciently known ancestor was a certain Otto Canella, Consul of Genoa in 1133, whose son was called Grimaldo.

It was a branch of this House of Grimaldi, which was to gain permanent possession of the sovereignty of Monaco after three centuries of struggle.

In 1270, the outpost of Genoese power at the frontiers of Provence, Monaco remained under the control of the authorities of the Republic until the end of the thirteenth century, but bitter civil warfare reigned between the aristocratic factions of Genoa from 1270 onwards. In the course of these internal struggles, Monaco became on several occasions the place of refuge of one of the great families engaged in the conflict, the Grimaldis. From these beginnings, and after two centuries of persevering effort, a new lordship, and a new State came into being.

In 1296, as a result of one of these party quarrels, the Guelphs and with them the Grimaldis were expelled from Genoa and took refuge in Provence. They had a small army, which they used against the fortress of Monaco.

On January 8, 1297, the Guelphs led by François Grimaldi, known as "Malizia" ("the Cunning"), seized the fortress. According to one chronicler, François Grimaldi penetrated the walls in the disguise of a Franciscan monk. This was the first capture of Monaco by the Grimaldis; the event is commemorated on their coat of arms where the supporters are two monks armed with swords.

In 1301, the Grimaldis lost control of Monaco. They were only to return thirty years later, thanks to the return to power of the Guelph party.

Charles Grimaldi occupied the Rock on September 12, 1331. In 1341, Charles I acquired the possessions of the Spinolas in Monaco. Historians consider him to be the real founder of the

Principality, to which he added land by purchasing the lordships of Menton and Roquebrune, both of which were to remain Monegasque until 1861. Charles I was the son of Rainier I and the father of Rainier II. These three Grimaldis occupied important positions at the court of the King of France and the Count of Provence. Rainier I, who commanded a fleet of galleys, was promoted Admiral of France by Philip the Fair and won a brilliant victory over the Flemish at Zeriksee in 1304. Charles I placed at the service of King Philip IV an army of crossbowmen who took part in the famous battle of Crecy in 1346, and his fleet took part in the siege of Calais. Rainier II, who never entered Monaco, had a glorious career as a sailor in the service of King John the Good and Queen Joan of Naples. His sons Ambrose, Antoine and John were lords of Monaco in 1419; after a division of the land between the three brothers, the Rock and the Condamine were allocated to John, who remained sole master of them until his death in 1454.

John I campaigned all his life for the independence of his lordship which the Genoese were not prepared to abandon. His son Catalan outlived his father by a mere three years, leaving as heiress a daughter who married a Grimaldi of the Antibes branch, Lambert. The successful policies of this lord led to the recognition of the independence of Monaco by King Charles VIII of France and the Duke of Savoy in 1489. It had thus taken nearly two centuries for the Grimaldis to establish their indisputable sovereignty over Monaco.

From then on, the attempts of the Genoese to recapture the fortress were limited to a siege which lasted several months and which was finally repulsed by the garrison in 1507. The independence of Monaco was again confirmed five years later by Louis XII who declared that the lordship was held by God and the sword. In 1512, Louis XII recognized by letters patent the independence of Monaco and a perpetual alliance with the King of France. This policy was continued by John II and Lucien until the death of the latter, assassinated in 1523 by his cousin Bartholomew Doria. He left only one son of tender years, Honoré, whose custody was given to his uncle Augustin, Bishop of Grasse, who was recognized as lord.

Augustin did not receive from François I the support that Charles VIII and Louis XII had given to his father and brothers. Following serious disagreements that arose between him and the French authorities, François I and the Emperor Charles V entered into negotiations, which ended in 1524 with Monaco being placed under the protection of Spain. This was an act whose consequences were to weigh heavily on the financial situation of the country for more than a century. Its instigator, before his death, was able to assess the gravity of the error which he had committed; the Spaniards only partly fulfilled their undertakings and the garrison which they placed in the fortress remained there almost entirely at the expense of the Monégasques.

At the death of his uncle Augustin in 1532, Honoré had not yet attained his majority. It was a Grimaldi from Genoa, Stephen, known as "the Governor" who was his guardian and had the government of the lordship granted to himself for his whole lifetime. The reign of Honoré was only peaceful towards its end; those of his two sons, Charles II and Hercules, who reigned one after the other, were also filled with intrigues and conflicts: Hercules was to perish assassinated in 1604. His son Honoré was still a minor; his custody was entrusted to his uncle the Prince of Valdetare until 1616. It was he who persuaded his nephew to take the title of "Prince" and "Lord of Monaco" (1612), titles which were recognized by the Spanish Court and passed on to his successors.

The reign of Honoré II witnessed the most brilliant period in the history of Monaco. As soon as he had assumed power, the young sovereign adopted as his policy an alliance with France. The discussions that began in 1630 lasted more than ten years. The Prince received the most favorable support from Cardinal Richelieu and he was assisted in Paris by his cousin John Henry Grimaldi, Marquis of Courbons and Lord of Cagnes and by Marshal de Vitry, the governor of Provence. In 1641, in Péronne, King Louis XIII signed a treaty providing Monaco with the friendly protection of France. This agreement confirmed the sovereignty of the

Principality, recognized the independence of the country and maintained its rights and privileges.

A French garrison was placed under the direct orders of the Prince who assumed command of it. There remained the problem of the expulsion of the Spanish garrison which continued to occupy the fortress. Several months later, Honoré II managed to organize as a fighting force a certain number of his subjects to whom he distributed arms; they succeeded in seizing the main posts, thus bringing about the capitulation of the Spaniards. During the course of the following year, the Prince was received at the French Court and obtained all sorts of honors and privileges. The lordships which had been given to his predecessors by Charles V in the Kingdom of Naples were replaced by those which were to become known in the Principality as the "French lands": the Duchy of Valentinois, the Viscount of Carlat in Auvergne and the Marquisate of Baux with the lordship of Saint-Rémy in Provence. Honoré II returned to the French court twice where he was magnificently entertained by Cardinal Mazarin. The young King Louis XIV was the godfather of his grandson, the future Prince Louis I.

The embellishment of the Prince's Palace during this reign was striking: first came the building of the South Wing, which contains the Great Apartments, today open to tourists. Honoré II gathered admirable art collections in his Palace: more than 700 paintings, many of which were signed by the greatest masters, were hung in the galleries; sumptuous furniture, precious tapestries, pieces of silverware and valuable ornaments provided a decor of great artistic worth which was the marvel of the eminent people whom the Prince invited to visit his Palace. Numerous events were staged during this reign, including those in the field of the arts such as the French and Italian ballets, balls were held and great religious ceremonies took place in the Church of Saint Nicholas.

Monaco: 1662 To 1815

Honoré II died in 1662. He had had only one son, Hercules, who had died as a result of an accident in 1651, leaving a son, Louis, and several daughters. Honoré II had the pleasure of witnessing the brilliant alliance of his grandson with Catherine-Charlotte, daughter of Marshal Gramont. The young princess occupied an important post at the French Court.

Her residence in Monaco was only short; however, she used it to found the Convent of the Visitation, which later became a college and today is the Albert I Grammar School.

She then returned to Paris and became Lady in Waiting to the Princess Palatine. Louis I, who had followed her, took part in the War of the United Provinces against England. At the head of his regiment, the Monaco Cavalry, he fought battles in Flanders and Franche Comté. He later returned to Monaco because of his poor health and it was there that Louis XIV came to entrust him with the embassy of the Holy See. His mission was to obtain the support of the Pope to ensure that the succession of the King of Spain, Charles II, would pass to the Dauphin, the son of Maria Theresa. The unheard magnificence, which he displayed in Rome, obliged him to empty the Palace of the riches that his grandfather Honoré II had gathered. He died in 1701 without having had to intervene in the Spanish succession.

He had had two sons by Charlotte de Gramont : Antoine, the elder, succeeded him and François-

Honoré became Archbishop of Besancon. Antoine was forty years old when he ascended the throne. He had spent a lot of time living in Paris where he had forged links with the great French aristocracy, in particular with the Duke of Orleans, the future Regent. He had a brilliant career in the army as Colonel of the Soisson Infantry Regiment. His considerable height and dynamic spirit earned him the nickname of "Goliath". In 1688, he had married Marie de Lorraine who belonged to one of the greatest families allied to the throne of France. She filled a splendid position at the French court and only rarely visited Monaco. In addition, because of his health, Antoine I hardly ever left Monaco. During the invasion of Provence by the Duke of Savoy in 1707, the Principality, in spite of its neutrality, had grounds for fearing invasion. Large-scale fortification work was undertaken by the Prince, including the tower "Oreillon" ("the Ear") which commands the ramp leading to the Palace and which was completed in 1708. The Principality remained on the alert until the Treaty of Utrecht, signed in 1713.

Antoine I maintained voluminous correspondence with the most well-known figures of his time; including with Marshall Tesse, which has been published. His great taste for music placed him in contact with François Couperin and André Cardinal Destouches, the directors of the Paris Opera.

In 1731 the male line of the Grimaldis of Monaco died out with Prince Antoine as Marie de Lorraine had only given him daughters. In 1715, he gave the eldest, Louis-Hippolyte, away in marriage to Jacques-François-Léonor de Matignon, heir of one of the most illustrious families of Normandy and owner of a great deal of land and possessor of many lordships ; he held the County of Torigni, the

Duchy of Estouteville and the Barony of Saint-Lô. Jacques de Matignon, as a result of arrangements made by the parents of his bride, gave up his name and coat of arms for those of the Grimaldis. Louis XIV agreed to confer on him the title of Duke of Valentinois.

On the death of his wife ten months later, he was recognized as Prince of Monaco with the title of Jacques I, then held the regency during the minority of his elder son, the future Honoré III, in favor of whom he abdicated on 7th November 1733. Jacques I lived out his days in semi-retirement devoting his time to the magnificent art collections assembled in his house in Paris, which is still known today under the same name, the Hotel Matignon, while it has become the official residence of the French Prime Minister.

Honoré III was to be Sovereign Prince of Monaco until 1795. During the first years of his reign, he had taken part in campaigns in Flanders, Rhine and the Low Countries and was promoted in 1748 to the rank of Field Marshal.

During the War of the Austrian Succession, from 1746 to 1747, Monaco was blockaded by the Austrian-Sardinian forces; the latter were repulsed after several months by the troops of Marshall de Belle-Isle. This was the only crisis of the reign, which ended in peace. The Prince spent more time in Paris and on his land in Normandy than in the Principality. He was, however, there during the summer of 1767 when the young Duke of York, the brother of King George III of England, on his way to Genoa, suddenly fell ill and had to be landed in the harbor of Monaco. He was immediately taken to the Palace but, in spite of the care and attention he was given, he died several days later. The

English Court expressed its deep gratitude to Honoré III for his hospitality. One may still visit the room in the finest of the great apartments of the Prince's Palace in which the Duke of York died.

The wedding of Honoré III with Marie-Catherine of Brignole-Sale was celebrated in 1757. The Brignole family was one of the richest and most powerful families in Italy.

The marriage, however, did not last long. Irritated by the social success of his wife in the entourage of the Prince de Condé, Honoré demanded and obtained a separation. Before the quarrel between the spouses, two sons had been born, Honoré, who was later to become Prince of Monaco, and Joseph. The elder married Louise d'Aumont Mazarin in 1776; as a result of this union the Sovereign's House acquired all the property left by Cardinal Mazarin to his niece Hortense Mancini, including the Duchy of Rethel, the Principality of Château-Porcien and many other estates.

The situation of the Princes and their subjects was therefore at its most brilliant when the French Revolution broke out. Thanks to the wise administration of the Governor, the Chevalier de Grimaldi, the people lived rather well in spite of the lack of resources in the territory of the Principality. Maritime commerce and the revenue arising from taxes levied on ships making their way to Italy contributed to a considerable extent to the economy of the country. The Princes, with their fiefs of Valentinois, in the Auvergne, Provence and their land in Normandy, enjoyed a large income which was made even larger by the contribution from the lordships in Alsace. All these sources of income were removed by the suppression of feudal rights voted by the French Constituent Assembly during the night of August 4, 1789.

Honoré III tried in vain to have his rights respected by invoking the Treaty of Péronne; on his death, which took place in 1795, his family found itself in dire financial straits.

In Monaco, two opposing parties came into being; one was the supporter of sovereignty. The other, the Party of the People, wanted to hand the government over to the people and its representatives.It was the latter who overcame this opposition.

The entry of French troops into the County of Nice hastened the establishment of the new order. On February 15, 1793, the Convention decided upon the incorporation of the Principality into France. First it was a canton, then the chief town of an arrondissement, which was later moved to San Remo.

All the riches of the Palace were dispersed the paintings and articles of artistic worth being sold at auctions. The Palace, after first being used to provide billets for officers and soldiers in transit, was converted into a hospital and then into a home for the poor.

Throughout the whole of the Revolution, the members of the Prince's family had undergone severe trials. First they were imprisoned and then freed, with the exception of Marie-Thérèse de Choiseul-Stainville, the wife of Prince Joseph (the second son of Honoré III) who perished on the scaffold. They found themselves in all sorts of difficulties and were obliged to sell nearly all their possessions. Two of them, Honoré-Gabriel and Florestan, served in the French army.

The situation changed completely after the abdication of Napoleon on May 30, 1814. The first

Treaty of Paris returned to the Principality all the advantages, which it had enjoyed before January 1, 1792. Prince Honoré IV, son of Honoré III, unable to assume power because of his poor health, nominated his brother Joseph to replace him but his son, Honoré-Gabriel, vigorously opposed this notion and his father, understanding his son's argument, passed him sovereignty. Honoré therefore returned to Monaco in March 1815. On his arrival in Cannes, he learned of the departure of Napoleon from Elba; he was arrested by General Cambronne and taken in the middle of the night to speak with Napoleon.

Monaco: 1815 To Present

After the final fall of the Empire, the second Treaty of Paris of November 20, 1815 placed the Principality under the protection of the King of Sardinia. A treaty was signed on Novemebr 8,

1817, with King Victor-Emmanuel I at Stupiniggi. The situation of Monaco resulting from this was much less advantageous than the alliance with the King of France. The state of the finances was more delicate, the resources of the country being very much reduced, the communes, parishes and hospitals burdened with debts.

Honoré-Gabriel, having become Prince Sovereign under the name of Honoré V, tried throughout his reign from 1819 to 1841 to remedy this state of affairs. The measures taken, although dictated by a very strong concern for the general interest, were not always happy and often alienated the population. There were several hostile demonstrations, in particular in Menton in 1833.

In 1841 upon the death of unmarried Honoré V, power passed to his brother Florestan. This Prince, passionately interested in literature and the theater, was unprepared for the exercise of power. Luckily, his wife, Caroline Gilbert of Lametz, daughter of a family with a bourgeois background, possessed remarkable intelligence and a very developed sense of business; she was a great help to him. The first measures taken to redress the difficult situation, which the decrees of Honoré V had created, had the effect of calming the people for the moment but was of short duration. Florestan and Caroline, however, made every effort to re-establish prosperity.

Serious disagreements then came to a head with the commune of Menton, the inhabitants having shown their desire for independence for some time. The King of Sardinia, Charles-Albert, had given a liberal constitution to his subjects and the people of Menton demanded a similar one for the Principality. The constitution, which Florestan offered them on two occasions, did not meet their approval; after the revolution of 1848 in France, the situation grew worse. Florestan and Caroline handed over all their powers to their son Charles. But it was too late to assuage the spirits of the people. On March 20, 1848, Menton and Roquebrune declared themselves to be free and independent townships. However, annexation by the Kingdom of Sardinia, in spite of the efforts of the Court of Turin, did not take place. The efforts of Florestan and, after his death in 1856, those of his son Charles III, were also unsuccessful. Troubles continued until the Treaty of Turin in 1860 which ceded to France the county of Nice and Savoy. Shortly after the Treaty of February 2, 1861, Charles III gave up his rights to France over Menton and Roquebrune. This treaty, which gave the Prince, an indemnity of four million francs for the loss of the two towns, guaranteed for him the independence of Monaco under his sole authority.

For the first time in three centuries, the independence of Monaco was formally recognized and freed from any link with a protecting power.

The Principality, reduced to one-twentieth of its territory, deprived of the revenue, which it drew from Roquebrune and Menton, found itself in a financially difficult situation. In order to meet the expense of administration and the cost of upkeep of the Court, it was imperative to find other sources of revenue apart from taxes whose rates could not be increased. In 1863 after several attempts to increase commercial activity, Charles III and his mother Princess Caroline had the idea of establishing a gaming house under the name of the Société des Bains de Mer. The concession was given in turn to two businessmen, neither of whom was able to manage the enterprise successfully. It was then that François Blanc, director of gaming at Homburg, who came to be called the Magician of

Monte Carlo, obtained the concession for fifty years. Under his enlightened management, the business developed to an extent, which was far beyond the most optimistic forecasts. Situated in an enchanting setting, the various establishments hotels, theater and casino of the Seabath Company attracted hosts of tourists from the very beginning, in spite of the difficulty of access to the Principality. Later, in 1868, when the railway line between Nice and Ventimiglia was completed, their number increased to remarkable figures. The economic growth of the Principality increased in a striking manner and at the same time the development of the town went ahead at an incredible pace. On the rocks of the Spelugues, the main establishment of the Seabath Company, the Casino, was quickly surrounded by luxury hotels and splendid buildings. This area changed its name in 1866 and in honor of Prince Charles assumed that of Monte Carlo.

Between 1866 and 1905 the Principality signed treaties relating to the extradition of wrong-doers with Italy, Belgium, France, the Netherlands, Russia, Switzerland, Austria, Hungary, Great Britain and Denmark as well as conventions on Legal Aid and Reciprocal Communication of Civil Status Deeds with Italy, Belgium and France. Monaco was also a signatory of several multilateral treaties such as the Paris Convention of 1883, the Berne Convention of 1886 and the Madrid Arrangement of 1891. At the same time, Monaco accredited Ministers or Chargés d'Affaires to Paris, the Vatican, Spain, Italy and Belgium. Charles III also increased the number of his consular agents.

Prince Charles III, living for most of his reign in his chateau of Marchais in Champagne, did not, however, neglect the direction of public business, aided by the enlightened advice of the lawyer Eynaud. It was to this Prince and his son, Prince Albert I, that Monaco owes its striking development, its reputation and its institutions.

Albert I succeeded his father in 1889. Until then he had devoted himself entirely to scientific research, which engrossed him. His discoveries in the fields of oceanography and paleontology won him a great reputation and a seat in the Academy of Sciences. It would take too long to list all his achievements; it suffices to recall that he was the founder of the Oceanographic Institute, which consists of the famous Museum inaugurated in 1910 and the establishment created in Paris to teach this science. We are indebted to him also for the Museum of Prehistoric Anthropology in Monaco and the Institute of Human Paleontology in Paris. In addition, in 1903 he founded the

International Institute of Peace with the task of "studying the means of resolving disagreements between nations by arbitration, propagating attachment to methods of harmonious agreement and removing hatred from the hearts of people".

In the field of the arts, activities undertaken during his reign won the Principality a magnificent reputation; the Opera, created in 1869, under the directorship of the eminent Raoul Gunsbourg, rapidly won international fame due to the superior quality of its performances and its creations, which were to become famous.

In 1869 Prince Albert married Marie-Victoire de Douglas-Hamilton. This union produced Prince Louis II who succeeded his father in 1922. Prince Louis II, a graduate of the Saint Cyr military college, enjoyed a career as an officer of colonial troops in Algeria. Having left the army, he returned to service life again during the 1914-1918 War and was promoted to the rank of general. The attempts of Prince Albert I to persuade the Kaiser to stop the war in 1914 unfortunately bore no fruit. On January 5, 1911, Prince Albert I gave Monaco a Constitution. With the consent of Prince Albert I, Prince Louis II married his daughter, Princess Charlotte, to Prince Pierre de Polignac. It was this marriage which produced in 1921 H.S.H. Princess Antoinette and in 1923 H.S.H. Prince Rainier III.

Joining the French Army as a volunteer during the Second World War, H.S.H. Prince Rainier III was mentioned in Brigade Orders with the award of the War Cross and in 1947 He received the Cross of the Legion of Honor, military division. In 1949, He succeeded His grandfather, Prince Louis II, to the throne.

On April 18, 1956, Prince Rainier married Miss Grace Patricia Kelly, who was born in Philadelphia on November 12, 1929. Their three children are: H.S.H. Princess Caroline, born in Monaco on January 23, 1957, H.S.H. Prince Albert, Heir to the Throne, Marquis of Baux, born in Monaco on March 14, 1958, and H.S.H. Princess Stephanie, born in Monaco on February 1, 1965.

During His 56-year reign, Prince Rainier maintained Monaco's political, economical and social stability and transformed this idyllic Riviera holiday spot into a thriving international financial, business, cultural and sports center and premier luxury tourist destination. He initiated many innovative infrastructure policies and oversaw the Principality's unique geographical extension and its exceptional economic development. In 1958, He opened up Monte-Carlo's seaboard and in 1965 launched the land reclamation project that extended Monaco's territory by 20 percent. Other major infrastructure projects included the Grimaldi Forum Monaco, a state-of-the-art conference and cultural center and the transformation of Port Hercule with a unique, semi-floating breakwater, installed in 2002, which allows for increased capacity and the docking of larger cruise ships. Light manufacturing and hi-tech commercial businesses found a home in the new Fontvieille district, bringing diversity to the Principality's economy. These economic advances continue to ensure Monaco's citizens and residents receive substantial social and cultural benefits.

He was dedicated to establishing the Principality's status in the international community in 1993 Monaco became the United Nations' 183rd Member State, and in 2004 it was admitted to the Council of Europe. As the leader of a prosperous democratic nation, He gained much international respect by offering His patronage and financial support to many social and humanitarian causes. His commitment to scientific and environmental issues stemmed from his passion of the sea and His legacy to the world's oceans includes thoughtful resource management practices and conservation techniques.

With the invaluable contribution of His beloved Princess Grace, Monaco became an international center for cultural and sporting events. Les Ballets de Monte-Carlo, the Monte-Carlo Philharmonic Orchestra, the Little Singers of Monaco, the Prince Pierre Foundation, the Princess Grace Foundation, the International Circus Festival, Spring Arts Festival, the Monaco Formula 1 Grand Prix and the Tennis Open are just some of the many initiatives that grew and prospered under His leadership.

On September 14, 1982, Princess Grace died as a result of a tragic motor car accident.

H.S.H. Prince Rainier, known as "The Builder Prince", passed away on April 6, 2005 in Monaco at the age of 81. The official ceremonies marking the enthronement of H.S.H. Prince Albert II took place in Monaco on July 12, 2005.

The Prince's Palace of Monaco

From ancient Greek times to the end of the Roman era, the rocky promontory and natural harbor of Monaco had been mentioned in the literature of the time because of their strategic location.

The palace began as a fortress when in 1191 the German Emperor Henry IV ceded the harbor and the rocky promontory to the Republic of Genoa on the condition that they build fortifications to combat piracy. Additional property was acquired from the Council of Peille and the monks at the Abbaye de Saint Pons and construction actually only began in June 1215 when Fulco de Castello, one of Genoa's most enterprising consuls, anchored his fleet of ships loaded with building supplies in the harbor. By then they were ready to trace the outlines of a rampart of thirty-seven sections and four buttressed towers connected with 8-meter to form a triangular boundary. Later a higher wall was erected and a second fortress was added on the port side entrance, none of which remains today.

Genoa played an important role in Europe of the 12th century and the Grimaldis were one of the aristocratic families of Genoa. The Genoese were traders throughout the Mid-East and the Orient and bankers who provided foreign sovereigns with funds, ships and armed soldiers. When the Holy

Roman Emperor Frederick II of Hohenstaufen challenged the authority of Pope Innocent IV, the Genoese divided into two parties: The Guelphs sided with the pope and the Ghibellines with the German Emperor. The Grimaldis belonged to the Guelps who were the defenders of the Pope. Conflicts between the two groups continued into the late 13th, when the Ghibellines won, they ousted the Guelphs—and the Grimaldis—from Genoa.

On the evening of January 8, 1297 Francois Grimaldi, nicknamed Malizia, disguised himself as a monk and asked for shelter for the night at the fortress in Monaco. The unwitting guard let him in and was killed and Francois, and with his men captured the fortress for the Grimaldis. The seizure of the fortress enabled Rainier Grimaldi to wage war on Genoa with France, who made him a French Admiral. However, it was Charles I, the son of Rainier, who is considered the first lord of Monaco in 1341. For 30 years the fortress was lost and won back several times. The Grimaldis acquired Menton in 1346 and Roquebrune in 1355 and Charles I installed a loyal garrison and strengthened the existing fortifications by expanding the ramparts and building a breakwater to protect the entrance to the port.

In the 15th century, Lambert continued to protect Monaco by building defenses around the 'rock' and installing a 400-man garrison. All this time, improvements were made to the fortress and it was slowly being transformed. The main three-story building, protected by high scalloped walls connecting the towers of Saint Marie, Milieu, and Midi was located on the east side where the Palace stands today. Between the first two towers and the front of the ramparts Lambert built a two-story building, whose rooms opened onto a balcony.

The Grimaldis have always fought to keep their land and sovereignty. In order to do so they have waged wars against Genoa, Pisa, Venice, Naples, France, Spain, Germany, England and the Earls of Provence. The cost of the sieges and fighting took a heavy toll on the fortifications, which were badly damaged during 1505 and 1507. The lords of Monaco also forged many diplomatic alliances in particular with their neighbor France. Finally in 1480 Lucien Grimaldi persuaded King Charles of France and the Duke of Savoy to recognize the independence of Monaco's.

As a consequence, by the reign of Honore I (1522 – 1581) the old fortress structures were transformed into the Palace, as we know it today. In the courtyard, architect Dominique Gallo designed a portico with two double-decked galleries, each with twelve arches, with white marble balustrades on the upper gallery, which is known as the

Gallerie d'Hercule. A new wing was constructed on one side of the courtyard and Genoese painter Lucas Cambiaso was commissioned to paint frescoes on the walls. Because defense could not be overlooked, a new tower was built reinforced with additional towers and a cistern under the courtyard was enlarged hold to 3963 gallons (15,000 cubic meters) of water to sustain 1000 soldiers for a 648-day siege. The interior of the cistern, which is 16 feet (5 meters) deep by 66 feet (20 meters) long and 262 feet (80 wide), resembles a church with a vaulted ceiling resting on nine massive pillars.

In 1633, the Spanish King permanently recognized the title of "Prince of Monaco" to replace the "Lord of Monaco", making Honore II the first Prince of Monaco. Prince Honore grew up in Milan and was influenced by the intellectual salons of Paris. Like his ancestors, he had a love of the arts and became a great collector of tapestries, silver, furniture and paintings. His collection of 700 pictures included works by Raphael, Durer, Titian, Michaelangelo, Rubens and other noted local artists. He hired Jacques Catone an architect of the time, to make spectacular improvements to the palace. He masked the Genoese towers by adding on the wing facing the square.

In the main courtyard, he extended the state apartments, which also concealed the Serravalle Tower behind the building erected on either side of the new Saint Jean Baptiste chapel. He then added the grand royal entrance leading into the courtyard. These improvements took 30 years to complete, but they made the Palace of Monaco one of the most remarkable royal residences of the 17th century.

Unfortunately the French Revolution significantly impacted the Palace and the Grimaldi reign. In January 1793 the National Convention ordered all occupied lands be governed by independent administrations based on those of France. This ordinance applied to the Principality. Thereafter the Palace was occupied and looted by the citizens of Monaco, Roquebrune and Menton. Monaco was downgraded to a mere cantonal seat and the name changed to Fort d'Hercule. The objects of Grimaldi wealth were sold at auction. The State Apartments were turned into a military hospital for the Italian army, the throne room was used as a kitchen and the rest of the Palace designated a Poorhouse.

In May of 1814 Monaco was returned to the Grimaldi family and initially placed under the continued protection of France. By this time, however, the Palace was in such a terrible condition that the part of the east wing on the Fontvieille side had to be demolished as well as the Pavillon des Bains. Standing now in this spot is the Napoleon Museum and Palace Archives.

It is Prince Rainier III, who is credited with restoring the greatest part of the lost glory of the Palace to its present splendid state.

Today, from June to October, the Palace is open to visitors. There they can see the royal courtyard paved with 3,000,000 white and colored pebbles formed into beautiful geometrical patterns. On exhibit are the 16th-century Genovese frescoes depicting scenes from mythological. The columns and the spectacular double-revolution staircase inspired by a staircase at Fontainebleau are done in Carrara marble.

The Sovereign Prince appears in the Gallery when receiving Monegasques at official events or for the presentation of a future prince or princess. But during official receptions and at the Christmas party for Monegasque children, the Prince welcomes his guests in the State Apartments.

These rooms are inlaid in marble with mosaic designs including the double R monogram of Prince Rainier III. The Florentine and Boulle furniture is from the reign of Francois I. The walls are draped in silk brocade and damask and hung with royal portraits executed by well-known artists. These portraits also document the prestigious marriages made with royal families such as Savoie-Lorraine, Matignon, Aumont-Mazarin

Economy

From a historical standpoint, a rapid survey leads to the conclusion that from the end of the Nineteenth century and the beginning of the Twentieth, the Public Authorities have encouraged the economic growth of the Principality and provided the framework for the development of private enterprise.

The economic activity of the principality takes place along four main lines:

Industrial activity, often little known, but an area which has undergone considerable development in less than a century. From 1906, when the State financed the construction of the first platform in Fontvieille, industrial firms such as the Monaco Brewery and companies involved in flour-milling and the manufacture of chocolate began to settle there. Over the course of the last twenty years, nearly 200,000 square meters of industrial floor-space has been built. The small area of Monaco's national territory leads to the setting of industrial premises in buildings which rise to thirteen floors.

The Government of the Principality has adopted an industrial policy which operates in favor the establishment of enterprises having a high capital gain factor but which do not create any pollution. The "chemical-pharmaceutical-cosmetics" sector appears to be the most numerous but companies working in the areas of plastic material processing and the manufacture of electrical and electronic equipment are also present.

Other sectors, while they are not on the same scale as those described above, bring renown, originality and technical performance to the Principality; they are to be found in particular in the sectors concerned with printing, electronic materials, textiles and garments.

Industrial activity is represented by 105 establishments and 3,500 jobs. In 2005, they generated approximately 8% of the total turnover generated in the Principality.

The Principality of Monaco today has a diversified industry and yet it is perfectly integrated into its setting and its environment.

Tourist activity is essentially connected with private tourism or business tourism. In 2001 this sector was responsible for 13% of the Monégasque economy. The hotel industry of the Principality has 2,616 hotel rooms with a total of 3,920 beds, most of which are in the four star category. The average occupation rate in the region was 58.39% in 2005 or in other words over 800,000 overnight stays and rose to 75.5% in 2006, which worked out at around 915,650 overnight stays.

Furthermore, the cruise industry plays an important role for the tourist activity of Monaco. In 2005, over 190 ships called into port bringing a total of 133,000 passengers to the microstate.

For several years, the public authorities have been making considerable efforts in the area of catering for business touristsas for instance the construction of the Grimaldi Forum which is a approximately 592,015 square feet congress center where 454 congresses were hosted in 2005. At present time, tourists coming to Monaco on business or for converences and seminars represent 30 % in terms of hotel occupancy.

The third sector includes tertiary activities which have been greatly developed over the course of recent years in the areas of banking and financial activities, and the establishment of head offices and offices of non-financial companies of international size.

The sector which has undergone the most spectacular growth is that of services. It produced, in 2005, around 44% of the turnover and its sphere of activity includes banks, insurance, consulting agencies (technical, commercial, financial and the like), auxiliary services and middlemen.

The fourth sector is that of commerce which represents 39% of the total turnover in 2005.

Finally, real estate activity plays an important role in the economy with 7% of Monégasque turnover, justifying research and determining the directions taken in the field of city planning.

The total turnover of the Principality rose from 3.25 thousand million francs in 1975 to 29 thousand million franks in 1990. In 2000, the Principality of Monaco produced a total turnover of 3.2 billion Euro and in 2005 it passed the 10 billion Euro mark with a turnover of 11 billion euro, which is a 12% increase compared to 2004.

In an uncertain and complex international environment, with the ever-enlightened encouragement of its Sovereign, the Principality of Monaco preserves its originality: without any natural resources and a tiny territory, it is developing and modernizing itself. A city of 32,000 inhabitants, it provides work for about 44,200 people, around 40,300 jobs are in the private sector and the rest of 3,900 in the public sector. Every day, 28,000 French and 6,000 Italians come into Monaco for work. The Principality makes efforts to manage its advantages in the best possible way with the constant aim of improving the quality of life so as to bring work and leisure together in a harmonious fashion.

Food

Food in Daily Life. Access to fresh, local produce and the sea has led to the development of a local cuisine and appreciation for good food. Monaco has many restaurants, and seafood is featured in many dishes. Daily eating habits reflect a Mediterranean heritage, and both French and Italian influences can be found in the local recipes. Breakfast is very small, but lunch and dinner often have several courses.

Food Customs at Ceremonial Occasions. Holidays such as Christmas, Holy Week before Easter, and Carnival before Lent are occasions for special food. Some traditional Monegasque dishes include brandamincium, salt cod pounded with garlic, oil, and cream surrounded by cardoons, edible Mediterranean plants, in white sauce; barba-Giuan, or "Uncle John," stuffed fritters; and fougasses, flat, crunchy biscuits sprinkled with sugared anise seeds and flavored with rum and orange-flower water.

Basic Economy. Tourism and related businesses are the main components of the Monegasque economy today. The tourist industry began when the famous casino was opened in Monte Carlo. Banking and financial activities are the second most important part of the economy. The industrial sector is small but significant and includes pharmaceuticals, cosmetics, flour-milling, and food products. Investment in real estate and business services make up the fourth most important sector of the economy. Foreign companies receive special investment incentives that have led many to open offices in the principality. Monaco does not impose an income tax on its residents and consequently has attracted corporate and individual investment. A significant financial services industry has developed as a result.

Land Tenure and Property. Due to Monaco's small size, the availability of land and private space has always been limited. Significant economic growth and an increase in population since 1950 have greatly augmented this problem, forcing developers to build multistoried structures very close together. An increase in tourism and the necessity for hotels have put an added strain on available space. Property is expensive both to buy and maintain, but Monaco's real estate business continues to thrive. To create additional space, the Monegasque government has had to find innovative ways to satisfy the demand for construction: the use of land reclaimed from the sea. The most recent of these is the neighborhood of Fontvieille.

Commercial Activities. Business related to tourism accounts for the majority of commercial activities. Hotels, restaurants, shops, gambling, and services related to Monaco's port provide both employment and revenue for the principality. The real estate business has also become an important commercial concern since 1970.

Major Industries. Industry did not begin to significantly develop until the 1950s, and consists entirely of light industry, with no obvious adverse effects on other parts of the economy or Monegasque society. The first industries, which developed at the beginning of the twentieth century, included a brewery, a chocolate factory, and a flour mill. The chemical, pharmaceutical, parapharmaceutical, and cosmetics industries all developed after World War II and today consist of twenty-three separate businesses—many of which are leaders in their sectors in Europe. Plastics, electronics, printing, textiles, and construction also are significant industries.

Trade. Recent figures place the estimated value of Monegasque imports at U.S. $415,300 and exports at approximately the same figure. Monaco does not publish economic figures including gross domestic product, although recent estimates put it at about U.S. $800 million. Exports include a variety of Monegasque products, and imports include agricultural products and manufactured and consumer goods. Some of Monaco's most important exports include: cosmetics, pharmaceuticals, clothing, small electronics, and paper products.

Division of Labor. Of the estimated thirty thousand jobs existing in Monaco, two-thirds of them are held by workers commuting from neighboring French or Italian towns along the coast. Seasonal tourist work also accounts for an increase in non-native

Monegasque workers to the principality, including workers who have immigrated to Europe from other parts of the world. Women make up slightly less than half the workforce, and recent statistics place unemployment at about 3.2 percent.

Social Stratification

Classes and Castes. Monaco's high average income and individual wealth, as well as its very small size, make it a country with minimal class distinctions. The principality's status as a tax haven make it an attractive place to establish residence for wealthy people from all over the world. A significant number of residents are from a variety of nationalities, and several are celebrities, helping to make Monaco synonymous with wealth, power and prestige the world over.

Symbols of Social Stratification. Overall Monaco has one of the highest standards of living in the world. Differences in social stratification are not immediately obvious. The principality's popularity as an exclusive resort and tax haven has led to the development of a very wealthy social class. Material symbols of wealth such as luxury goods, expensive cars, and exclusive shops are visible everywhere. Monaco's coastal position has also made it a popular port for luxury yachts. The tourist industry necessitates a large workforce, as do Monaco's light industrial concerns, but more than half the people employed in these sectors do not live in Monaco.

Political Life

Government. Until 1910, the Principality of Monaco was governed by an absolute monarchy. In 1911 Prince Albert I promulgated the first constitution, which was modified in 1917. It was modified again in 1933 by Prince Louis II, and other reforms were made by Prince Rainier III in 1962. Monaco's refusal to impost tax on its residents and international businesses led to a severe crisis with France in 1962. This crisis led to a compromise in which it was agreed that French citizens with less than five years of residence in Monaco would be taxed at French rates and companies doing more than 25 percent of their business outside the principality. Another result of the crisis was the creation of a new, more liberal constitution ad the restoration of the National Council. The constitution provides that executive power is under the authority of the reigning prince. Succession to the throne passes to the direct and legitimate descendants of the prince, with male descendants taking precedence over female.

The prince represents Monaco in its foreign relations and signs and ratifies treaties. The prince nominates a Council of Government, consisting of a minister of state and three government councilors, one each for finance and economy, the interior, and public works and social affairs. The Minister of State is a French Citizen, appointed by the prince, and selected for a three-year term a from a group of senior French civil servants selected by the French government. The Minister of State is in charge of foreign relations and, as the prince's representative, directs executive services, the police and the Council of Government. Under the Council of Government's authority is the eighteen-member National Council. Members of the National Council are elected for five years by direct vote based on a system of proportional representation. Eligible voters must be over the age of twenty-one and hold Monegasque citizenship for more than five years. The new constitution of 1962 gave the right to vote to women, established a Supreme Court to guarantee fundamental rights, and abolished the death penalty.

Leadership and Political Officials. Local affairs are directed by the Communal Council which administers the principality's four quarters: Monaco-Ville, La Condamine, Monte Carlo, and Fontvieille. The Council of the Crown consists of seven members holding Monégasque nationality who are nominated by the prince. The president and three members are selected by the sovereign: the others are selected by the national Council. Current government officials include: the Chief of State, Prince Rainier III; the Minister of State, Michel Leveque; the Council of Government, ministers for: the Interior, Finance, and Economic Affairs, Public Works and Social Affairs, National Council President, President of the Supreme Court, and the Director of Judicial Services.

Social Problems and Control. Due to its small population and unique economic situation, Monaco does not face many of the social problems that larger countries must deal with, such as violent crime and poverty. After going through a period of economic growth and industrial development following World War II, a primary concern is the principality's ability to sustain its economy, attract new investments, and maintain the quality of life for its citizens. Current social problems include managing industrial growth and tourism, environmental concerns, and maintaining the quality of life. Alcoholism and illegal drug abuse are present but not widespread. Monaco has a very low crime rate, in part due to the high number of law enforcement officials in relation to the total population and the high standard of living. Widespread use of security cameras throughout the principality also further discourage open criminal activity.

Excluding private security, there are around 400 permanent police officers, 95 percent of whom are French. Legal power belongs to the Sovereign, presently Prince Rainier III, who delegates full exercise of it to the courts and tribunals. The independence of the judges is guaranteed by the constitution. Monaco's legal organization includes all degrees of jurisdiction: a Court of First Instance, a Court of Appeal, a Higher Court of Appeal and a Criminal Court. There are also tribunals with specific competence, such as the Work Tribunal, the Rent Arbitration Commission, and the Higher Arbitration Court, for collective work disputes. The Supreme Court is at the top of the principality's legal organization.

Military Activity. Monaco does not have a military, although it does have a small police force. The French government is responsible for Monaco's defense.

Social Welfare and Change Programs
The government efficiently manages several social welfare and change programs. Some current programs include creating more affordable housing for workers by reclaiming land from the sea for new construction and promotion of Monegasque culture, brought about by a revived interest in the principality's history. Consequently,

Monegasque language classes have now been instituted in all elementary schools. The Monegasque government also ensures generous pensions, maternity leave, vacation time, and welfare programs for all citizens.

Nongovernmental Organizations and Other Associations

Monaco has many nongovernmental organizations and cultural, academic, and professional associations. Among these are the Permanent International Association of Navigation Conventions, the International Committee of Military Medicine and Pharmacy, the Scientific Community for Oceanic Research, the International Music Council, the International Union for the Conservation of Nature, and the International Union of the History and Philosophy of Sciences. Monaco joined the United Nations in 1993 and is an active participant. Other intergovernmental organizations of which Monaco is a member include Interpol, UNESCO, and WHO. The International Hydrographic Bureau has its headquarters in Monaco.

The People, Culture and Tradition

The cultural climate of the Principality developed rapidly in the seventeenth century with the encouragement of Prince Honoré III. Under Prince Pierre of Monaco during the first half of the twentieth century, Monaco was a meeting place for all the greatest artists of the time.

Following this lengthy art patronage tradition, H.S.H. Prince Rainier III includes culture and arts as one of his principal concerns. For over fifty years of His reign, H.S.H. Prince Rainier III has encouraged all forms of arts from music to literature.

Under His auspices, Monaco's Music Academy was founded in 1956. The National Philharmonic Orchestra initiated summer performances in the Palace's Courtyard of Honor. In memory of His Father, Prince Pierre de Monaco, H.S.H. Prince Rainier III instituted the Foundation Prince Pierre, which assigns the Prince Pierre Literary Prize (since 1951), the Musical Composition Prize (since 1960), and the Contemporary Art International Prize (since 1983). His H.S.H. Prince Rainier III created the Directorate of Cultural Affairs in 1966, responsible for coordinating and encouraging all cultural activities of the Principality including the Spring Arts Festival, the Baroque Music Week, and the International Circus Festival.

Under His direction, Monaco's cultural institutions have also gained international prestige. The Little Singers of Monaco went on their first tour around the world in 1973.

The Prince receives support from His family in His interest in the arts. The late Princess Grace was at the origin of many developments, such as The Princess Grace Irish Library. In 1964, the Princess Grace of Monaco Foundation was created to support the performing arts. The Dance Academy Princess Grace, directed by Marika Besobrasova, is an offshoot of this foundation.

H.S.H. the Princess of Hanover reformed the academy in 1985 to launch the Les Ballets de Monte-Carlo. The Princess also presides over the Spring Arts Festival.

Today, Monaco counts several major cultural ambassadors:

The Monte-Carlo Philharmonic Orchestra

The first permanent orchestra established in 1863 came into its own with the opening of the Garnier Palace in 1879. In 1953 it became known as the

National Orchestra of the Monte-Carlo Opera, and it was renamed the Monte-Carlo Philharmonic Orchestra in 1979. Many great conductors of this century, from Richard Strauss to Toscanini and Leonard Berstein to Lorin Maazel, have led the orchestra in concert. The Orchestra's Music Directors have included Paul Paray, Louis Fremaux, Igor Markevitch, Lovro von Matacic, Laurence Foster and James DePreist. Today, the Artistic Director and Conductor in chief of the Monte-Carlo Philharmonic Orchestra is Marek Janowski.

Opera of Monte-Carlo
Since its creation in 1879, the Opera of Monte-Carlo has gained international fame, playing a key role in promoting the most beautiful voices to the rest of Europe. The Opera of Monte-Carlo secured a reputation for artistic innovation. Authors such as Bizet, Franck or Massenet wrote some of their

works for the Monéguasque Opera. Regularly, the Opera goes on tours to play works of its repertoire.

Les Ballets de Monte-Carlo

After founding the Academy, which bears her name, Princess Grace wished to revive an old tradition by inviting George Balanchine, Serge Lifar and J.B. Cerrone, a Monégasque who directed the "Harkness Ballet" and founded the "Houston Ballet". Remembering her mother's wishes, H.R.H. the Princess of Hanover created the new Monte-Carlo Ballet, the management of which she first entrusted to Ghislaine Thesmar and Pierre Lacotte. Today Jean-Marc Genestie is responsible for the Administrative Direction and Jean-Christophe Maillot is the Choreographer. With enthusiasm and competence, they are striving together to raise the Company to the highest international level.

The Little Singers of Monaco

These young voices carry on a tradition from the reign of Prince Antoine I in the early eighteenth century, when an ensemble of children's voices sang the liturgies in the Palatine Chapel. In 1973, the Government of the Principality asked the late Philippe Debat, whose son Pierre is the current Chapel Master, to carry out a musical mission in every country of the world with a choir of children's voices only. Prince Rainier III affectionately called this choir of 26 boys "My Little Singing Ambassadors".

Traditions

Religious and civil traditions have been upheld for centuries in the Principality. They are sometimes linked, rites and ceremonies being accompanied by popular festivities, but the former are more firmly anchored in the collective memory of Monégasques than the latter. They are an integral and exclusive part of the social, cultural and moral heritage.

Saint Devote

January 27

Once upon a time right at the beginning of the 4th century … there was, on the Island of Corsica, then a Roman province, a cruel governor who persecuted Christians. It was under these circumstances that Dévote, who had vowed her life to the service of God, was arrested, imprisoned and tortured. She died without denying her faith and her martyred corpse was placed by pious hands in a boat leaving for Africa where she would find, they believed, Christian burial.

But in the very early hours of the crossing, a storm arose. And from the mouth of Saint Dévote a dove made its appearance. The storm then abated. The dove guided the boat right up to the coast of

Monaco where it ran aground at the entrance to the little valley of the Gaumates ... on a bush bearing early blossoms.

The body of Dévote was piously received by the small Christian community, which lived in the neighborhood. It is on this day, the sixth of the calends of February for us, 27th January of the year 312 of our era, that Saint Dévote took under her protection Monaco and its inhabitants. A rustic oratory marked the place of her tomb. The faithful, residents and sailors passing through Monaco, went there in greater and greater numbers to venerate the relics of the Saint ... and the first miracles took place.

It was then that an evil idea took possession of the mind of an unscrupulous man who, in the dead of night, stole the relics of the Saint with the intention of taking them beyond the seas and selling their powers.

The intended sacrilege was cut short as Providence was watching. A group of fishermen witnessed the robbery and with a few strokes of their oars, made much more powerful by their anger, overtook the thief and his precious plunder. Brought back on to the beach, the thief's boat was burnt as an expiatory sacrifice. During the sieges, which Monaco underwent in the sixteenth century, the Italian Wars and the Wars of Religion, the relics of the Saint were exposed on the ramparts, inspiring the defenders and spreading terror among the besiegers.

That heroic age has now passed away. However, the cult of Saint Dévote still remains strong in the Principality.

Positive proof of this can be seen by attending the ceremonies and events which take place, as soon as night falls, around and inside the Church dedicated to St. Dévote which was constructed in the reign of Prince Charles III on the site of the original oratory.

Every year on this date, there is a torchlight procession, a religious ceremony and blessing followed by the setting on fire of a boat on a pyre decorated with olive, pine and laurel branches; a picturesque symbolic copy of the boat which the Monégasques burnt in the past to efface all trace of an unpardonable crime !

The evening finishes with a firework display given over the waters of the harbor of Monaco, facing the outlet of the little valley of the Gaumates where the long association between Dévote and the Monégasques started.

The life of Saint Dévote was superbly sung by the Monégasque poet Louis Notari (1879-1961). His poem "The Legend of Saint Dévote" was the starting-point, now more than half a century ago, of a sort of rebirth of the Monégasque tongue. This dialect, with its full-flavored intonations and its amazingly rich vocabulary, has since then been the subject of university theses both in France and elsewhere. It is included in the syllabus of the various schools of the Principality.

Holy Week Processions

The origin of the religious traditions of Holy Week may probably be traced back to the time of the Crusades, when survivors of these distant expeditions to the Holy Land introduced the Christians of the West to the rites of their brothers of the East. Accounts of the first Good Friday Processions can be found in Monaco from the thirteenth century. This ceremony, however, did not take on its full significance until the foundation by Prince Honoré II in 1639 of the Venerable Brotherhood of the Black Penitents of Mercy.

Since that time, this Brotherhood, whose members are Monégasques of all ages and conditions, brought together in the spirit of serene piety and disinterested love of one's neighbors, each year organizes on the evening of Good Friday, the Procession of the Dead Christ, a traveling evocation complete with all the characters, real or imaginary, of the main Stations of the Cross.

Carnival

The tradition of the carnival in Monaco probably goes back to the fifteenth century. The carnival, the period between the Sunday of Epiphany and Ash Wednesday, was the opportunity people to enjoy themselves before the long and austere period of Lent.

Young and less young disguised themselves as best they could in old clothes, formed processions, exchanged bawdy cat calls and, holding a large piece of cloth by the corners, threw up into the air an ungainly dummy figure stuffed with straw and rags.

Fights with projectiles, which were often far from harmless rotten eggs, chickpeas, gravel, oranges and lemons enlivened the passing of the procession, which usually finished with the burning of the dummy amid general merriment. After this, weather permitting, there was dancing at the corner of the streets or in the fields to the shrill sound of makeshift instruments.

The tradition of the Carnival has been revived over the last thirty years or so with "Sciaratù". Organized by the Roca-Club, this comic procession with its floats, disguises, enormous dummy heads, fights with confetti and dancing in the open air, which rounds off the evening, takes place in the height of summer to the delight of tourists in search of local color.

Saint John's Day

June 23-24

On the eve of Saint John's day, 23rd June, when the gardens of Monaco are ablaze under the setting sun, Monégasques mindful of the customs of their country assemble on the Palace Square.

There are folk groups, surrounding the Palladienne, Monaco's own folk group, a dynamic gathering of young people, wearing the costumes of the past, singing, dancing and playing the mandolin charmingly. Groups come from France, Italy and Spain to take part in the Monégasques' Saint John festival.

In the Palace chapel, dedicated to Saint John the Baptist himself, the Prince's Family attend a service which is also attended by several privileged people such as the Presidents of the Tradition Associations, together with their flags.

At the end of this ceremony, two footmen of the Sovereign' s Household, each dressed in fine livery and carrying a burning torch, set alight a bonfire set up in the center of the Square.

The people in the crowd applaud with all their hearts. Airs of bygone times accompany farandoles around the flames over which the boldest leap with a single bound.

On June 24, Saint John's Day, the Feast moves from Monaco-Ville to Monte Carlo.

A procession forms up on the Place des Moulins (Mill Square) where the old olive presses used to operate.

The folk groups form a guard of honor around "Little Saint John" and his lamb. The procession, accompanied by music of its own making reaches the Church of Saint Charles in the parish of Monte Carlo.

After a religious service, the procession returns to the Place des Moulins. A bonfire is set up, the Monégasque national anthem is played and then, the popular and religious feast combined, the great ball of Saint John commences in the open air and continues until late at night.

Saint Roman

August 8-9

After Saint Dévote, Saint Roman is the most popular and most venerated saint in the Principality.

The veneration by the Monégasques of this Roman legionary, who suffered martyrdom on August 9,

258 in the reign of the Emperor Valerian, goes back to the sixteenth century when a relic of Saint Roman was entrusted to the Terrazzani family who had a chapel built in which to lay it.

For several centuries, the Feast of Saint Roman took place at the hamlet of les Moulins ("the Mills") near to the old chapel.

Around 1880, the festivities moved to Monaco-Ville. Today, with the support of the Committee of the Feasts of Saint Roman, we still dance and enjoy cool drinks in the month of August under the foliage of the hundred-year-old trees of the Saint Martin gardens.

Monégasque National Holiday

November 19The Monégasque National Day, or "Fête du Prince", is celebrated every November 19th.

The tradition dates back to the reign of Prince Charles III. The date used to vary to coincide with the Patron Saint's Day of the reigning Prince. However, when The Sovereign Prince Albert II succeeded his father in 2005, he decided to maintain the National Day on November 19th, St. Rainier of Arezzo's day, in his honor.

National Day is a time of joy and pride for the Country when the traditions and ideals of the community are celebrated. Monégasques and residents of The Principality attend various events, showing their support and affection for The Prince and his family. Windows, balconies, shops and streets are adorned with the red and white colors of the national flag.

In the days leading up to the "Fête du Prince", the whole country takes part in a range of activities culminating in a fireworks display in Port Hercule on November 18th. The Princely Family personally delivers care packages to the Monaco Red Cross and to senior citizens. The Prince presides over several medal ceremonies, bestowing prestigious distinctions such as Ordre des Grimaldi (Order of Grimaldi), Ordre de Saint Charles (Order of St Charles), and Mérite Culturel (Cultural Merit) among others.

On November 19, the Prince and his family, along with officials and nationals, attend a morning Thanksgiving mass at the Cathedral, followed by a parade of Monaco's official corps (police and fire departments, Prince's Guards, etc) on the Palace Square.

Festivities conclude with an opera gala evening at the Monte Carlo Opera or the Grimaldi Forum in the presence of the Princely Family.

Monégasque Christmas

In Monaco, until the end of the last century, Christmas Eve was the occasion when all the members of a family would gather at their parents' home to perform, as a preliminary to the evening meal, the rite of the olive branch. Before sitting down, the youngest of the guests, or the oldest, soaked an olive branch in a glass of old wine. He approached the fireplace where a great fire of pine and laurel branches burned and with his little branch traced the sign of the Cross while pronouncing a few words on the virtues of the olive tree, a source of all kinds of good things. After this, everybody in turn wet his lips in the glass of wine serving as an aperitif before the gala dinner whose main dish was an enormous "brandamincium", a Monégasque dish of salt cod pounded up with garlic, oil and cream, surrounded by "cardu", cardoon in white sauce; "barba-

Giuan", literally "Uncle John", stuffed fritters and "fougasses" flat crunchy biscuits sprinkled with sugared aniseed colored red and white, flavored with several drops of rum and orange-flower water.

On the table covered with a splendid cloth lay a round loaf of bread "u pan de Natale" (the Christmas loaf) on which four walnuts formed a Cross surrounded by several olive twigs.

From this Christmas of olden times, there are still in existence, besides Midnight Mass in the Cathedral, "Barba-Giuan", "fougasses" and "u pan de Natale" to be found at some bakeries in the Principality.

Numerous traditions, which, lapsed today but perhaps only temporarily forgotten, bore witness right up to the last century either to the religious spirit or joy of living of the Monégasques.

The traditions of Saint Blaise, very popular among country people: the peasants came in procession, often on the backs of donkeys, from the plain of the Condamine or its neighboring hills, to have the seeds of their future crops blessed together with several handfuls of figs; these latter had the power when drunk in an infusion of curing tonsillitis and seasonal colds.

The tradition of the "Mays" with, from the first to the last of this month marking the height of Spring, dances ("farandoles") round a Maypole, decorated with flowers and red and white ribbons the Monégasque colors set up in the very center of the Palace Square.

The tradition of the "pignata" ball, organized on the first Sunday of Lent, which takes its name from the cooking pot which members of the crowd, their eyes blindfolded, tried to break at intervals with heavy blows of their sticks.

The tradition of the "ciaraviyù" (the Monégasque form of the French word" charivari" meaning "row or racket") that consisted of providing the most unharmonious serenade possible, continuing all night long, under the windows of newlyweds when they formed a far too disparate couple.

Plus many others which the National Committee of Monégasque Traditions, established in 1924, is trying to revive as it has already revived, to quote only one example, the tradition of Saint Nicolas, the patron saint of good children, on December 8.

Sports

The Principality, the crossroads of the world of sport with its world-renowned events the Monte-Carlo Rally, the Grand Prix, the International Tennis matches and so on is also a think-tank for the official bodies which govern sports …

Towards the end of the nineteenth century there was already in existence in the Principality a "Regatta Committee" which was replaced in 1888, on the initiative of a group of a dozen Monégasques, by a sports association established to promote, encourage and develop water-borne sports such as sailing and rowing. The first Monégasque sports association was formed under the name of the "Société des Régates de Monaco" which is today the "Société Nautique".

In addition, the Principality of Monaco, rejoicing and full of euphoria as a result of the extraordinary success of the new town of Monte Carlo and banking on the future with confidence, gave its support to the still embryonic motorized sports :

1877, the Tennis Master Series had their debut in Monte-Carlo, being now one of the most important international Tennis events.

1904, the first speedboat meeting;

1910, the take-off from the Quai Antoine I of a biplane, as fragile as a child's toy, but at the controls of which Henri Rougier was to realize the exploit of flying over the nearest spurs of the Alpes-Maritimes;

1913, the first "hydro-aeroplane" meeting (ancestor of the seaplane). Similarly, other sports including golf (with the opening in 1910 of the first course on the slopes of Mont Agel), tennis, fencing, shooting, boxing, football and athletics all took wing and on the eve of the 1914-1918 war, the sporting activities of the Principality were already exemplary and were to continue :

1928, opening of the Monte Carlo Country Club and Monte Carlo Beach with its Olympic-standard swimming-pool;

1929, the first automobile Grand Prize race;

1939, the inauguration, by Prince Louis II, of the stadium which bears his name and which was immediately used to stage the last University World Games before the Second World War.

With the Liberation, sport came into its own again. Its development in all fields was at lightning pace and from then on Monaco possessed a range of sports clubs and federations recognised by international bodies.

Working in Monaco

No foreigner may occupy a private salaried position in Monaco unless he possesses a work permit which only allows him to occupy the post mentioned, as any change of employer, trade or profession entails requesting a new permit.

Formalities of engagement carried out through:

Direction Du Travail Et Des Affaires Sociales

Service De L'emploi

(The Employment Office)

"La Frégate"

2, Rue Princesse Antoinette

Monaco, MC 98000

Principality of Monaco

Tel: +377 93 15 80 00

Fax: +377 93 15 89 74

The employer who wishes to engage or re-engage an employee of foreign nationality must obtain permission in writing before this latter starts work.

This permission may, in addition, be refused if people in the same profession or specialization who have priority are registered with the

Employment Office on the lists of those seeking work.

The following order of priority is observed:

➤ People having Monégasque nationality;

➤ Foreigners married to a Monégasque woman and not legally separated and foreigners born to a Monégasque parent;

➤ Foreigners living in Monaco who have already held a job there.

These priorities are meant to protect the local labor force.

In order to allow their application, employers are required to declare any job vacancy to the Employment Office, which will send to them, within four days, a candidate or candidates for the post.

In the absence of a person having priority, the employer may put forward the application of an employee.

The employee must hold:

➤ If he lives in the Principality, a valid Monégasque residence card;

➤ If he lives in France, a French identity card or a valid residence document;

➤ If he lives neither in Monaco nor in France, the applicant must conform to the rules concerning the entry and residence of foreigners.

In this latter case, the employer must establish a work contract for a foreigner worker. This contract, after approval by the Employment Office, will make it possible to obtain the visa required for settlement in the Principality from the French consular authorities of the country of origin.

The formalities for the issue of a work permit are only launched after the issue of a Monégasque residence permit.

From information supplied by the employer, he will receive a pre-printed request for engagement and issue of a work permit which he is required to complete and return as quickly as possible to the Employment Office.

Permission to engage someone is only issued if the person concerned passes a free medical examination carried out by the Employment Medical Service.

Living in Monaco

Conditions required for entry and residence in the Principality for a period not exceeding three months

Any person of foreign nationality who wishes to enter Monégasque territory and stay there for a period not exceeding three months must have the document (passport, travel or identity document) required for entry into French territory.

French subjects must merely be holders of the national identity card.

No other formality is required of foreigners who wish to travel to Monaco.

Conditions required for entry and settlement in Monaco
Any foreigner, except French subjects, who whishes to live in Monaco for a period longer than three months or establish residence there, must be the holder of a settlement visa.

To obtain a settlement visa, the person concerned must apply to the French General Consulate nearest to his domicile.

Supplied with this visa, every foreigner over sixteen years of age is required to request within eight days of his arrival in the Principality of Monaco a resident's card from the Foreigners' Section of the Directorate of the Police Service (Tel: +377 93 15 30 15).

Opening a Business

The Steps

1. To enter Monaco, all foreigners must have proof of identity (national identity card or passport).

2. Anyone planning to stay in Monaco for more than three months or establish residency must obtain a long-term visa (French consulates handle visa arrangements for the Principality), as well as a residence permit (carte de séjour) which is available from Monégasque police headquarters (Direction de la Sûreté Publique) upon arrival.

3. Anyone wishing to work in Monaco must also obtain a work permit (permis de travail).

4. To establish a company in Monaco you must present to the Economic Expansion Department (Direction de l'Expansion Economique) the following documents:

Notarized statutes or private deeds which have been registered with the Tax Department (Direction des Services Fiscaux);

Registration forms detailing partners' civil status and a description of the company's registered office on Monégasque territory

5. To establish an agency or administrative office of a foreign company on Monégasque territory, you must send to the Minister of State (Ministre d'Etat) an application which includes:

Two certified copies of the company's articles of association;

A certificate proving the company's registration in the country of origin;

A Board of Directors' directive to open an office in Monaco;

A copy of annual accounts for three preceding years;

A description of the premises where the office will be located;

Details of the appointment of a responsible representative in Monaco;

A report on the structure of the company: date of creation, main activities, countries of operation, personnel, etc.

Information forms are obtainable from the Economic Expansion Department. Documents in a language other than French must be accompanied by a French translation.

All applications for an administrative office in Monaco are subject to approval by the sovereign government of the Principality.

6. To create a commercial company in Monaco, you must obtain preliminary approval from the sovereign government to operate commercial, craft, industrial or service activities. Authorization from the Minister of State is obtained by submitting:

A formal request on stamped paper addressed to the Minister of State;

A certificate proving a clean police record issued within the last three months;

A description of the office premises;

Information about the applicants' civil status (birth, marriage, divorce, etc.);

Diplomas and references;

Completed information forms from the Economic Expansion Department.

Such a business may be operated either by the proprietor or by a manager (for whom authorization must be obtained).

Entry and Residence in Monaco

To enter Monaco, or reside there either temporarily or for a considerable length of time, all non-French citizens must follow certain simple procedures:

1. All non-French citizens wishing to visit Monaco for less than three months must possess the same documents that are required to visit France. For U.S. citizens that means a valid passport.

2. Any non-French citizen wishing to stay in Monaco for more than three months must obtain the following documents:

A long-term visa, which is available from French consular offices in the United States.

A "carte de séjour" or residence permit, which is

obtained from the Monégasque police headquarters upon arrival. Applicants will be asked to provide detailed information about themselves, and their immediate family's civil status. They will also be asked to show documents concerning their accommodations in the Principality, such as lease agreements or ownership deeds for property.

Applicants also must show proof of employment or professional activity if they intend to work while in Monaco. If they do not intend to work, they must show sufficient financial means of existence without working.

3. Foreigners may apply for temporary residence (a one-year resident permit which can be renewed twice, each time for one year); as an ordinary resident (a three-year resident permit which can be renewed twice, each time for three years); or as a privileged resident (valid for ten years, and

renewable after administrative inquiry has determined that residence is actual).

4. All non-French citizens wishing to work in Monaco must obtain a "permis de travail" or work permit from the Department of Employment by first showing a residence permit or work contract. The work permit allows an individual to perform only the work for which it was issued.

Buying real estate in Monaco

Real estate transactions take place in great freedom. The only formality is the deed executed and authenticated by a notary which guarantees the validity of the transaction both for the purchaser and the vendor. Any individual and legal entity, whatever his nationality, may become the purchaser of a piece of real estate in the Principality.

The cost per square meter (approximately 10.7 square feet) for an apartment located in a new building varies between 45,000 francs and 80,000 francs ($ 8,036 and $ 14,286 / 1USD = 5,6 FF).

Individual

An individual must produce documents providing proof of his identity and civil status:

Monégasque residence permit or national identity card or passport;

Family record book if married under the joint estate system;

Marriage contract, if one was drawn up.

Legal entity

A legal entity must produce the following documents in French:

The articles and memorandum of association of the company;

A copy of the relevant entry from the Register of

Companies less than three months old;

The minutes of the general meeting approving the purchase of the property;

Notarized power of attorney authorizing a person to represent the company and to conclude the transaction.

If there is a translation into French, it must be supplied by a sworn or authorized translator. When these documents come from abroad, they must be certified as being a true copy of the original by the nearest Monégasque consulate. Please contact the New York consulate to receive a listing of your nearest consulate.

Notaries

The purchase and sale of an item of real estate must of necessity be carried out using the services of a notary.

The notary is a legal official who works within the framework of a learned profession; he is authorized to deal with all deeds and contracts to which the parties concerned must or wish to give the legal status which is associated with documents of the public authorities. For this reason, he certifies their date, keeps them in safe custody and delivers engrossed and authentic copies of them.

He is required to prepare legal instruments and deeds which, in the context of the transfer of a piece of real estate, provides the necessary guarantees for the purchaser. In fact, in addition to his professional liability being involved, he ensures the performance or supervises the formalities essential to the execution of the documents he prepares. In particular, he is required to register the legal instrument or deed at the Mortgage Registry in Monaco, which enables him to check that there is "…No mention of a mortgage taken out on the property sold whether this was done by the vendor or previous owners."

The cost of the notarized documents consists of: The notary's fees: The percentage is applied to the total before sales tax: Above 20,000 francs 1.5%, to which are added small supplementary expenses (copies, stamps, etc.).

The registration fees

General system: 7.5% (registration 6.5% and entry 1%). These fees are calculated on the price stated or the market value if the latter is higher.

Special system: Entry 1% plus VAT. This system applies to transactions taking place at the same time as the construction or delivery of buildings.

Protection of intellectual property in Monaco
There is no country in Europe that takes the protection of industrial intellectual property more

seriously than Monaco. This protection is available to all American citizens as well as any individual or business domiciliated or established on the Monégasque territory, or any territory of a country bound by the Paris Convention for the protection of industrial property rights.

At the national level

Property rights may be obtained in three areas:

Patents

The maximum duration of patent protection issued in Monaco is 20 years, with the application process offering secrecy (access only to the applicant and his/her legal inheritors) for about two years.

Published information about the grant of a patent is limited to: name and address (or registered office) of the applicant, patent number, date of filing and grant, title of the invention, its classification and reference to priorities claimed.

Patents are granted without governmental guarantee or research as to the patentable nature or precedence.

Industrial design

Industrial design protection is offered for ten years, with the possibility of five ten-year renewals, for a total protection of fifty years.

Generally, applications for industrial design protection are made in the form of drawings, photographs or illustrations.

If the applicant has submitted an international design under the Hague Agreement, there is no need for further formalities within the Principality in order to be protected on Monégasque territory if Monaco is designated in the international deposit.

Industrial design protection is issued without governmental search and all applicants are urged to carry out their own by consulting the register of granted designs.

Trademarks

The duration for trademark protection is ten years, with multiple renewals possible.

Published information about patented trademarks includes: Whether it is a figurative trademark or specific graphic representation, date of deposit, patent number, name and address of owner, categories in which protection is required, description of goods and services, reference to priorities claimed, if any.

At the international level

Monégasque residents may apply for international patents, providing protection in some 80 countries covered through the World Intellectual Property Organization, or a European patent, providing protection in the countries of the European Union.

The Principality of Monaco is a signatory of the following international agreements:

Paris Convention for the Protection of Industrial Property Rights;

Berne Convention;

Madrid Arrangement for the International Registration of Trademarks;

Hague Agreement for the International Deposit of Industrial Designs;

Convention Establishing the World Intellectual Property Organization;

Patent Cooperation Treaty;

European Patents Convention

Gender Roles and Statuses

Monaco has a Mediterranean, Roman Catholic culture emphasizing the family. Until the second half of the twentieth century, women's roles revolved principally around family and household.

Women were not active in politics until the 1960s when they first received the vote. Although fewer women than men are employed outside the home, Monegasque women work in a variety of fields and are politically active.

Marriage, Family, and Kinship

Not withstanding its status as a cosmopolitan resort, Monegasque society is based on centuries-old traditions. Immediate and extended family are the basic social units. Marriage is considered an important family event and the divorce rate is low, with less than a quarter of marriages ending in divorce.

Marriage. Marriage is an important family event, Church weddings, held according to Roman Catholic traditions, are popular. A civil ceremony, held at the city hall, is also required even when a religious ceremony is organized. Some couples choose only to have the civil ceremony.

Domestic Unit. The domestic unit consists of immediate family members. Before industrialization after World War II, the domestic unit also included extended family such as grandparents and other elderly relatives. The low divorce rate and general affluence help contribute to a stable average domestic unit in Monaco. Monegasque social activities frequently revolve around family events and gatherings.

Inheritance. Inheritance laws are based on those of France.

Socialization

Infant Care. Monaco provides excellent maternity and infant care. Women are guaranteed several months of maternity leave and there are high quality, low cost day care centers and nurseries available. National health and education programs ensure that Monegasque families have complete early childhood support and care.

Child Rearing and Education. A national health service and an excellent public education system provide Monegasque children with high-quality, low-cost education and with health care from infancy through adolescence. Monaco's small size, unique history, and high standard of living have helped the principality avoid many of the child social problems that face larger countries. The traditional Monegasque culture, based on family and kinship ties, has changed with twentieth-century industrialization and growth, but child welfare remains important. Grandparents often help in caring for young children, particularly when both parents work.

Education is compulsory from ages of six to sixteen. School curricula are identical to those of France but also include the study of Monegasque history, the institutions of the principality, and the Monegasque language. There are four public primary schools for study up to age fourteen and three specialized high schools: Lycée Albert I, the Technical Lycée of Monte Carlo, and the Charles II College. There are also four private schools through the high school level.

Higher Education. Monaco does not have a university, although there are several specialized institutions of higher learning, including the Rainier III Academy of Music and the Nursing School at the Princess Grace Hospital Complex. Monaco's literacy rate is 99 percent.

Etiquette

Etiquette in Monaco is influenced by the country's unusual blending of roles as an international tax haven, exclusive resort destination in combination with the Monegasque traditions. The Monegasque are proud of the country's history and residents strive to maintain the quality of life that exists there. The principality attracts people from a variety of nationalities who are nevertheless united by a high level of personal wealth. The rules of etiquette are much like those found in France with an emphasis on respect for privacy. The royal family of Monaco, the Grimaldi, frequently attract the attention of the press. Monaco's royal family became a popular subject of tabloid journalism when the American actress Grace Kelly married Prince Rainier III. Discretion and privacy are still emphasized in Monaco.

Religion

Religious Beliefs. Roman Catholicism is the state religion, although freedom of worship is guaranteed by Article 23 of the Constitution. However, 95 percent of the population claims to be Roman Catholic.

Religious Practitioners. Most Monegasque are Roman Catholic and the church plays an important role in Monegasque traditions, particularly on feast days and special holidays. Church attendance is not as high as a century ago and it is difficult to estimate the exact number of practicing Catholics.

Rituals and Holy Places. There are several traditional festivals and rituals in Monaco. Saint Devote, the patron saint of Monaco, is venerated in a ritual held on 27 January every year. A torchlight procession, a religious ceremony and blessing mark the day that Saint Dévoe is believed to have arrived in Monaco. Other religious rituals and ceremonies are held during Holy Week before Easter, and on the feast days of Saint Roman, 9 August, Saint John, 23 June and Saint Blaise.

Death and the Afterlife. Monegasque beliefs about death and the afterlife are in accordance with the teachings of the Roman Catholic church.

Medicine and Health Care

Monaco has a government-supported health system that provides high-quality medical care to all its citizens. Life expectancy is placed at 74 years for males and 81 for females. Infant mortality rate is approximately 7 per 1000 births. Monaco's birth-rate exceeds the number of deaths per year. For specialized care of serious care of serious health problems Monaco's residents may seek care in larger medical centers, such as the hospital in Nice.

Secular Celebrations

National Day, 19 November, celebrates Monaco's independence as a principality. A parade, a thanksgiving Mass held in the cathedral, and special events are organized. Other important celebrations have religious origins. The Feast of Saint Devote, the patron saint of Monaco, is celebrated on 27 January. The festival of Saint John, on 24 June, is another important Monegasque holiday. Religious holidays are celebrated with the closing of businesses, special church services, and traditional customs. The National Committee of Monegasque Traditions, established in 1924, is dedicated to the preservation and revival of Monegasque folk traditions and festivals.

The Arts and Humanities

Support for the Arts. The Monegasque government actively supports the arts, cultural institutions, and the humanities through a variety of programs and events. The Prince Pierre Foundation was founded to encourage culture in the letters and the arts, by the creation and awarding of prizes. These

awards include the Grand Literary Prize, created in 1951; the Prince Rainier III Prize for Musical Composition, founded in 1960; and the International Contemporary Art Prize, awarded for the first time in 1965. The Princess Grace Foundation was established in 1964 with the aim of promoting charitable activities and provides support for the Princess Grace Dance Academy. Recent investments in the arts and humanities include the creation of a Cultural and Exhibition Center, which will contain an auditorium and other performance and event areas on the site of the old Centenary Hall. The Monte Carlo Ballet and the Monte Carlo Opera are world-renowned. The

Monte Carlo Ballet gained international fame in the 1920s when the choreographer Sergey Diaghilev was based there with his Ballets Russes. Monaco is also home to the International Circus Festival held every February and the International Fireworks held in July. The Grand Prix de Monaco, a Formula 1 car race held in the streets of Monte Carlo, is one of the principality's most famous cultural events and attracts thousands of spectators.

Literature. The Great Literary Prize recognizes outstanding literary works annually. The Princess Grace Irish Library was established recently to hold a collection of over 8,000 volumes related to Irish history, culture and writing, in both Irish and English languages.

Graphic Arts. The Prince Pierre Foundation annually awards the International Prize for Art, established in 1965, to recognize outstanding achievement in the visual arts. The Municipal School of Decorative Arts provides education in the visual arts.

Performance Arts. The Monte Carlo Philharmonic Orchestra was established in 1863 and found its permanent home in the Garnier Palace in 1879. The Monte Carlo Ballet and the Monte Carlo Opera are internationally acclaimed. Since 1892 the Monte Carlo Opera has occupied Garnier Hall, named after its architect, who also designed the Paris Opera House. Many premier performances have been staged at the Monte Carlo Opera, including Sergei Diaghilev's *Ballets Russes* in the 1920s. The International Circus Festival is also held annually in Monaco.

The State of Physical and Social Sciences

Monaco is particularly well known for its activity in the marine science field. The Oceanographic Museum, formerly directed by Jacques Cousteau, is the most famous institution devoted to marine science in the world. The Scientific Community for Oceanic Research is based in Monaco, and numerous other scientific and academic societies also have branch offices in the principality. Monaco's history of supporting oceanic and scientific studies dates to the 1860s when Prince Albert pursued his scientific interests by conducting numerous maritime expeditions. Throughout the twentieth century, Monaco has promoted scientific research. The Prehistory and Speleological Association was formed in 1951 and in 1960 Prince Rainier III inaugurated the Museum of Prehistoric Anthropology. Prince Rainier is also the president of the International Commission for the Scientific Exploration of the Mediterranean.

The Scientific Center of Monaco is host to a variety of activities including seismological, meteorological, and radioactivity studies. The Monaco Underwater Reserve, consisting of almost 50 hectares, was established by the Monégasque Association for the Protection of Nature to provide a protected environment for a wide variety of marine life. In 1971 the "Albert I of Monaco" Prize for Oceanography was created to recognize outstanding research.

Tourism

A miniscule city-state situated on the French Riviera in Western Europe, Monaco is the second smallest country in the world. Officially known as the Principality of Monaco, the country shares borders with France on three sides, with its western coast opening out into the Mediterranean Sea. Monaco makes up for its small size with its larger than life attitude, oozing with glamour and opulence. Be it the luxurious yachts dotting the harbour, the numerous celebrities flocking the country for its lavishness, or the remarkable events and festivals hosted by the country all around the year, every part of Monaco screams hedonism.

The history of Monaco can be traced back to the Grimaldi family who ruled Monaco since 1297. Over the centuries that followed, Monaco prospered as a major maritime port, as well as a strategic naval base for the European military powers. Following the French Revolution, Monaco was annexed by France. According to the Franco-Monegasque treaty of 1861, Monaco was placed under French guardianship, but retained its independence. Since 1911, Monaco has been a constitutional monarchy, with the Sovereign Prince of Monaco being the head of state.

The majority of the population in Monaco comprises of Roman Catholics, whereas the remainder is made up of Anglican and Jewish minorities. French is the official language of Monaco. Italian is spoken by the country's sizeable Italian community while English is also spoken by residents belonging to Irish, Canadian, British or

American decent. Monegasque, the traditional native language, is spoken by a minority of the population. Monaco enjoys a mild climate throughout the year, with hot, dry summers and wet, mild winters.

If you're looking to bask in the best of Monaco, epic annual events like Formula 1 Grand Prix and the Tennis Master Series won't let you down. The country even hosts other iconic festivals such as the Monte Carlo Opera, the Spring Arts Festival, the Monaco International Non Violent Film Festival, and more.

Monaco sightseeing and Ctivities.

Travel guide - attractions, sights, nature and touristic places

The length of this principality is less than 2 kilometers, but that doesn't prevent it from being an internationally famous tourist destination. Monaco is distinguished by fine weather all year round as on average only 65 days a year have poor weather. Top class casinos, luxury hotels and unforgettable night life have made Monaco a popular resort for many people.

Monte Carlo Casino remains, probably, the most famous landmark in Monaco. The prominent casino is located in the Monte Carlo quarter. The entrance and ballrooms of the building are important architectural landmarks. The casino regularly hosts important events, such as the European Poker tour Grand Final. As stakes in this casino are usually very high, it is recommended to visit it in the morning and simply observe the building. The Grand Theatre de Monte Carlo, which is a ballet and an opera house, is open in the same building. The backyard of the building is the location of a beautiful garden with stunning views of the seaside.

Cathedral of Monaco is another popular tourist site. The façade of the beautiful church is nicely adorned with palm trees. Don't forget to make a walk at the waterfront and observe beautiful yachts that are docked there. Monaco has always attracted the wealthiest people in the world, and many of arrive using private yachts, so it's possible to see most luxury ships and make many memorable photos.

Monaco beaches are another signature attraction of the principality. There are special beaches for families with children with full monitoring, free public beaches, paid beaches and closed private beaches. Beaches with entering fee often sell pricey water and drinks, so it's a good idea to buy some water beforehand. Shopping is a no less popular activity in Monaco, so it's possible to find boutiques of nearly all popular European designers there.

Monaco is a popular destination, so there's no wonder why many important events take place there. The Grand Prix Monaco is one of them. The Formula One race takes place there every year in May. In January, travelers are welcome to attend International Circus Festival that gathers best performers from all over the world. March is the time for the Rose Ball, a famous fundraising event. Every year thousands of roses are used to decorate the Salle des Etoiles for the event. The annual Spring Arts Festival takes place in Monaco in April and includes dancing performances, arts exhibitions, music concerts and more.

History and Entertainment

Monaco is a place for elite recreation. There are the best hotels and restaurants on the Cote d'Azur. The integral symbol of the tiny country is the famous casino called Monte-Carlo. It will be interesting even for non-gamblers to visit this casino. It has long gained a status of the historical attraction visited by a lot of celebrities. It attracts with its historical atmosphere and luxury. Every evening, the grand entertainment program is organized for visitors.

During the year, there are a lot of interesting festivals held in Monaco. One of the most curious fests is an exhibition of fashionable yachts. The guests can board some yachts and appraise their luxurious design. In January, the annual International Circus Festival is held, during which you can watch performances of the best circus artists in the world. In May, the International Florist Competition is held. At this time, the city is decorated by charming flower beds and compositions of live flowers. There are also significant sports events, among which the Formula 1 Grand Prix and Monte Carlo motor rally are especially interesting.

Monte Carlo

Monte Carlo Sightseeing and Activities

what to see. Complete travel guide

Monaco is the capital of the Principality of Monaco. It is located on the French Riviera near the Italian border at the foot of the French Maritime Alps. In the south the microstate is washed by the Mediterranean Sea. The Principality of Monaco consists of several merged cities - Monaco (the old city), Monte Carlo (a shopping center and a location of numerous theaters, cinemas, casinos and other entertainment venues), La Condamine (a business center and a port) and Fontvieille (an industrial area). The principality is managed by the Grimaldi family, the oldest European princely family.

It is very simple to reach Monaco by train from Menton and Nice. A train ride along the coast will provide you with fabulous views of the sea and beaches. If you plan to go to Monaco by car, do not forget that parking is outrageously expensive there. Because of its small size, the city and all of its sights can be conveniently visited on foot. It will take you approximately half a day to explore the city and its most important sights, unless you make an indefinite pause at a game table in a casino or decide to wait until a member of the princely family waves a hand to you.

Prince's Palace.

The mandatory sightseeing program includes a visit to Monaco Prince's Palace . In summer, when the prince's family is away, the palace is open to tourists. When there's a flag over the palace, this is a sign that the prince is currently in the palace. Most of the items, which are usually visited there, date to the XVI century, and some of them - even to the XIII century. The palace is gorgeous outside. However, an incredible number of tourists can scare anyone. Thousands of sensation hunters want only one thing - they hope to see one of the members of the princely family in one of the windows of the south-west wing of the palace. On one side the Prince's Palace is surrounded by a beautiful park that leads to the sea. Walk in this park, and you will reach Musée Océanographique (The Oceanographic Museum) . In this park you will find beautiful flower beds with amazing plants. The park offers a magnificent view of the sea and the city. However, don't even plan to relax, even a little, in this beautiful corner of nature. Every minute crowds of tourists will pass you by. Typical bus excursion groups led by guides, who usually hold an umbrella or a sign in their hands, will not allow you to enjoy the beauty and harmony of the nature.

Casino in Monte Carlo.

Casino in Monte Carlo is another stop in the

mandatory excursion program. The wonderful casino was built by Charles Garnier in 1878. By the way, this building is a prototype of the famous Paris Opera. There is a huge square with lots of flowers in front of the casino. This is the best place to make magnificent pictures of this wonderful building. Before you go inside the casino, stand near the entrance a bit and watch luxury limos arrive one by one. Starting from early evening, an infinite chain of posh cars drives slowly to the casino. The cars, led by personal drivers, bring very rich players to the casino.

The rich enter the building, and the door is closed behind them tightly. Very few of these people appear in public halls, where thousands of ordinary tourists try their luck, sitting in front of slot machines or playing roulette at rather small tables. Here, everything looks different. Celebrities and millionaires are welcomed by a handshake and are brought to salons privés, where ordinary people are not allowed to enter. Mere mortals can get there only if two conditions are met. First, they pay for entering, and, second, they strictly follow the rules of the dress code. However, visiting this casino is a great idea not only because of the luxury building and famous players, but also because of its beautiful gardens.

Holidays in Monaco.

If you go to Monaco during the tourist season, you will be constantly surrounded by a crowd of tourists when you're in the old town, in the casino, or in front of the Prince's Palace. Is there, however, at least a small place in the city where one can relax a bit? If you go to the very east of the city, you will be delighted with peace and tranquility of a small beach. Unfortunately, the sun sets too fast and is soon hidden behind huge apartment buildings. The road to the beach goes through a Japanese garden. Fortunately, this little piece of Japan does not enjoy the attention of numerous tourists like other parts of the city. The north-west of the city is the location of Jardin Exotique. The exotic garden was laid out in 1933. You will hardly find privacy there, but you will certainly see unusual cacti and other tropical plants. There is one more great reason to visit this exotic garden located higher than the city and the sea, the garden provides truly magnificent views.

Everyone should visit Monaco at least once. Even if you're not interested in the Prince's Palace, then at least go to see the casino and the incredible auto show in the street in front of it. The city will leave a truly unforgettable impression, if you arrive in late May when the Monaco Grand Prix Formula 1 takes place there. Probably, you will not see much of the actual racing, but you will certainly experience an incredible atmosphere of racing. Afternoon is the best time to walk in Monaco. It is also wiser to spend the night in the neighboring French towns, where hotels rates are almost a half cheaper. An incredible number of tourists are the only negative factor. You will simply not find a place in Côte d'Azur with so many crowds of tourists as in Monaco. If in Nice, Cannes and St Tropez tourists are spread evenly in a large area, in Monaco they are concentrated on a narrow strip of land.

Famiy and Kids Favourites in Monte Carlo

Family trip to Monte Carlo with children.
Ideas on where to go with your child
Monte Carlo is not considered one of the best destinations for traveling with children. That is completely understandable as the city has become internationally famous for its casinos and nighttime entertainment for adults. However, there are still interesting culture and

entertainment venues in Monte Carlo, a visit to which can excite the whole family, and the Oceanographic Museum of Monaco is one of these places. This museum is distinguished by the awesome design. There is a giant aquarium with numerous colorful fish and an interesting hall with skeletons and models of prehistoric marine animals. It is allowed to touch some exhibits, and, as a rule, children love to do that. Once the excursion is over, visitors are recommended to go up to the roof of the building and enjoy views of the city from the observation deck.

Travelers, who enjoy walking in silent and picturesque places, simply cannot fail to fall in love with the Japanese Gardens. It is an incredibly beautiful Japan inspired garden with various exotic plants, numerous benches, and summer houses, beautiful parkways and bridges that are perfect for walking. There is a traditional pond with fish that is like a magnet for children. The park is suitable for relaxation even on a rainy day as there are special roofed pavilions. The entrance to the park is free.

If you plan to visit Monte Carlo in summer, don't forget to spend a day on the picturesque Larvotto Beach. The flat and sandy beach is perfect for sunbathing and relaxing with small children. Here they can enjoy different water-based entertaining activities, make sand castles, play beach sports, and order signature desserts in charming cafes located nearby. There are several well-equipped playgrounds for children and a beautiful park nearby.

The small Jardin du Casino Garden is another wonderful place for relaxation with children. The incredibly beautiful garden has become home for various exotic plants and countless palm trees. Pond remains the main attraction point for children in Jardin du Casino because there are many fish and ducks there, and children love to feed them. In the evening, it is always very calm and peaceful in the park, so even travelers with babies and toddlers can relax comfortably there.

There is a small zoo in Monte Carlo, Jardin des animalier, and families should not forget to include it into their excursion program. The zoo is not big, but the collection of animals present in it is quite diversified. There are behemoths, rare breeds of mountain goats, all-time favorite meerkats, turkeys, tapirs, and even kangaroos. The pavilion with talking parrots is traditionally very popular with children. The talking animals never cease to amaze small guests.

When it comes to describing family-friendly entertainment centers, NiBox should be mentioned first. The large entertainment complex can easily fascinate the whole family. In NiBox, there are playgrounds, rooms for small children, numerous arcade machines and simulators for older children, a bowling club and even charming cafes that are perfect for taking some rest after active pastime. In Monte Carlo, there are suitable entertainments for fans of beach rest, walking addicts and people who cannot imagine a vacation without shopping and visiting various fascinating places

Monte Carlo Cuisine and Restaurant

Cuisine of Monte Carlo for gourmets. Places for dinner best restaurants

Gourmet travellers will never be bored in Monte Carlo as the choice of gastronomic facilities here is truly very diverse. Le Pistou restaurant serves to its guests popular Mediterranean cuisine. Large choice of appetizers and an amazing selection of wines and desserts - Le Pistou is a great place for rest. Le Cafe De Paris restaurant cooks French cuisine. The elegant interior gives this restaurant its own unique charm. The opening of the restaurant took place in 1962. It is considered one of the oldest and most prestigious restaurants in the city.

Continue your exploration of culinary delights of French cuisine available in the restaurant named Le Louis XV. A glass of rare sparkling wine will become a perfect complement to seafood specialties of the restaurant. Fans of Asian cuisine will surely enjoy the meals that are served in Le Fuji restaurant. Soups with seafood, noodles with spicy sauce, sushi and, of course, the traditional sake the restaurant's chefs always try to impress visitors with new and original dishes. Don't forget to try the original author's dishes that are available in Le Grill restaurant. Dishes of French cuisine make up the basis of the restaurant's menu, but they are prepared in accordance with special recipes. Fried sea fish and meat dishes are the most popular choices among visitors.

Le Vistamar restaurant specializes in seafood. Among the dishes present in its menu you can find rarest delicacies. Stuffed seahorses, lobsters, shrimp skewers with vegetables and spices the food here is a true delight for fans of culinary. Blue Bay is an elegant restaurant that offers to its guests widest choice of international cuisine dishes. Blue Bay has its own wine cellar, so the connoisseurs of this drink have an opportunity to try rare and collectible varieties of wine.

Gastronomic traditions of France and Italy have pretty much shaped the formation of the regional cuisine. For many years, Bouillabaisse soup has been the most popular first-course dish in the region. The recipe of this soup has French roots. Bouillabaisse can contain different varieties of fish, but it always comes with garlic sauce. Saffron remains the key spice of the soup. Local restaurants usually serve Bouillabaisse with crispy croutons.

In Monte Carlo, all fans of seafood will be delighted with the choice of interesting dishes. For example, Anchoyade an unusual puree made of anchovies and capers, which has a very distinctive and original taste. The most popular dish with cod is called Stockfish. The fish is usually served with a special sauce that contains tomato paste and white wine. Travelers interested in savory meat dishes should consider ordering Porchetta in one of the restaurants specializing in the national cuisine. Porchetta is a stuffed suckling pig that is cooked in accordance with historical culinary traditions. It always has a very eye-catching serving.

Local chefs also cook many delicious lamb dishes. For example, the spicy lamb roll that usually contains numerous spices and herbs. Haven at Monte Carlo is the location of some of the best national cuisine restaurants. It is a great place to try various popular snacks and dishes that have won love and dedication of locals. Experienced foodies recommend visiting this part of Monte Carlo to try Barbajuan appetizer. The original dish will please travelers with its affordable price and unique taste. Barbajuan contains rice with cheese, spinach, and onion. Despite the fact that all the ingredients are simple and affordable, the appetizer is very delicious.

Socca pancakes are also a popular local snack. These fragrant pancakes are made of chickpea and flour. Local people also like Bruschetta, a traditional Italian snack. Bruschetta is a sandwich with crispy toast, cheese, olives, and tomatoes. Anchovies are one of the key ingredients of local Bruschetta. The choice of desserts is also amazing. Many local desserts and pastries contain fruits. The national cuisine widely uses dried and pickled fruits. It is also possible to buy mouthwatering dried figs and dates at local markets, as well as various nuts.

Almond cookies remain one of the most popular desserts in Monte Carlo. Travelers are also recommended to try delicious white and black nougat that can be made with different ingredients. When it comes to describing drinks that one is better to try exclusively in Monte Carlo, it is important to mention Pastis anise spirit. There are also several varieties of locally produced beer with La Segurane being the most famous one.

Finally, do not neglect La Blanche de Nice. It is a very interesting drink that contains coriander and orange zest

Monte Carlo Tradition and lifestyle

Colors of Monte Carlo - traditions, festivals, mentality and lifestyle

Millions of tourists from all over the world travel to Monaco to discover the fabulous Principality, located between the majestic Alps and the azure of the Mediterranean Sea. Monaco is one of the smallest, most exotic, most interesting and famous cities in Europe. The Principality of Monaco is a tiny and densely populated state, with the smallest constitutional monarchy in the world and indigenous population called Monegasque. Here they enjoy a lot of privileges, for example, they do not pay taxes. Moreover, Monaco's inhabitants have the special attitude to the family values and traditions. To celebrate holidays outside the house, leaving the family alone - is an unthinkable thing. It is customary to gather at a big table together, especially in the main religious celebrations.

In case Monaco has charmed you and now you are thinking about purchasing the real estate - keep in mind that here it costs crazy money. Of course, you can win this money in one of the Monaco's casinos, where the initial bet is only $ 10. Thus, a large fortune is not required to attract participation in this incendiary game, which attracts the attention of gamblers and successful people from all over the world. For all that, the local people are forbidden to play casinos at all. This is the city with crowds of tourists and active traffic, pebble beaches and sharp drops of depth near the shore. Here, you will not find infrastructure and entertainment for children. And if the child is too active or noisy, the parents be aware: residents and guests of Monaco are very zealous for their peace and comfort.

Monaco is a very cheerful and bright country. There is an incredible number of holidays, festivals, competitions of European and world level, which are an integral part of the Monaco's lifestyle. Whenever you come to this country, you will have a great chance to get to an interesting event, festival or contest which are dedicated to different topics and will satisfy any tastes. Every year, you can have fun at the International Fair and visit the Championship of Controlled Ship Models. In December, the opening of the ballet season. Residents also start the preparations for New Year's, Christmas and other festive holidays; all the city and streets are in decorations, as well as shopping centers, restaurants. Having arrived in Monaco in January, you can become a participant of The Monte-Carlo International Circus Festival and be imbued with extravaganza rally. In February, for connoisseurs and lovers of television art is the International Television Festival.

In March, you can get to the colorful opening of the Opera House and the Festival of Jugglers. But April is the most "festive" month. During this month, numerous events are taking place here, such as the Monaco Rose Ball, International Dog Show, Festival of Modern Sculpture, Monte Carlo Open and that is not even the end of the list. Residents of Monaco and fans of racing competitions from other countries are looking forward to May. The most glorious and famous Grand Prix of the world-famous Formula One takes place in May. This is the most difficult and prestigious race in the world championship. The race runs along the Monte Carlo track, and the audience is in close proximity to the passing cars.

This is incredible excitement, admiration for the masters of racing and cars. By the way, the museum of cars - a collection of old and most famous cars will be very interesting for you. In summer, you have the opportunity to join events such as the Monte-Carlo International Fireworks Festival and the Monaco Red Cross Ball. September is the month of sport. You can enjoy the delightful regatta called Rendez-Vous de Septembre, and the Grand Prix in athletics. From 27 to 30 September, here in Monaco, you will have awesome opportunity to watch the Monaco Yacht Show. Every possible representative of the industry, from designers to engineers and from brokers to office workers gather here as well. This exhibition is the most famous in the world and is located only on luxury yachts. It is also unique, as only yachts with a length exceeding 25 meters are represented here.

November 19 in the Principality people celebrate celebrated the most important holiday in the country - the National Day of Monaco. On this day, all of Monaco "dresses" in the colors of the national flag - red and white. The Monegasques express their devotion to the prince and his family. And the family of the prince participates in official events from morning till night. The morning begins with a solemn mass in the Monegasque language in the Cathedral of the Holy Virgin. The day ends in the opera of Monte Carlo, where all members of the princely family are again present at the play. This holiday with all its traditions and features reminds of the glorious past of Monaco.

Monte Carlo Cultural Sights to Visit

Culture of Monte Carlo. Places to visit - old town, temples, theaters, museums and palaces

The beautiful Palace Square and the princely palace located on it remain one of the main attractions of Monte Carlo. Every day thousands of tourists gather on the square to watch the ceremonial changing of the palace's guards. This ritual has become a symbol of the city, whose residents are very sensitive to the traditions and culture. Cathedral of Monaco is another striking architectural landmark of this place. It was built on the site of an old church in 1875. The first religious building on the site of the cathedral appeared in the 13th century. A beautiful ancient organ and a massive throne made of white marble have become the main ornaments of the cathedral.

Of course, there are more original excursion objects in Monte Carlo. Japanese garden is one of them. Located near the coastline, this is a large project created by talented designers and florists. In addition to plants of wondrous beauty, the garden is decorated with miniature waterfalls, bamboo fences, and stones - just like in a real Japanese garden. There is also a cozy tea house in the garden. This is one of the most attractive and charming places in the city.

Fans of excursions should not forget to visit the world-famous Cousteau museum, which was founded in 1899. The main exhibit of the museum is a huge aquarium, in which the museum's visitors will find a rich collection of inhabitants of the sea. Besides this, here are housed the collections of exhibits that tell about the work of the great explorer and oceanographer. Prince's Palace also hosts the museum of Napoleon, which is home to priceless historical documents from the First Empire. An excursion in the museum will be greatly enjoyed by numismatists and philatelists - old stamps and coins make up a significant part of the museum's exposition.

Old Antoine Fort is an interesting place of attraction not only to fans of walks in historical sites, but also to fans of theater. In 1953 the fort underwent a massive reconstruction, after which a beautiful theater was opened in it. Today the picturesque open-air arena can seat up to 350 spectators at a time. There is an unusual 'decoration' on the theater's stage - the pyramid made of cannonballs, which reminds visitors of the past of the military fortress. A high observation tower is among those buildings that have survived since ancient times. Nowadays it is equipped with a special playground for tourists.

Monte Carlo is not only a favorite place for celebrities, but also the preferred place when it comes to shooting films, where "effectiveness" and luxury are so needed. As a result, luxury hotels like Casino de Monte-Carlo often became a place for shooting "Bond" so you can see places from the familiar footage from movies such as "Never Say Never", "Golden Eye" and "Casino Royale". "Grace of Monaco", a film about the life of the Princess of Monaco, Grace Kelly, (in a year, she starred in the movie "To Catch a Thief" by Alfred Hitchcock) was shot here. Almost every corner of Monte Carlo can boast of this fact. Hotel de Paris also appeared in the movie "Iron Man 2".

By the way, Grace Kelly is loved and honored here. The city has a monument to the Hollywood actress, who managed to become the princess of Monaco as a result of her cold aristocratic beauty, and the church in which she is buried (Cathédrale de Monaco), is a favorite place of pilgrimage for tourists precisely due to this fact. You find too that Prince Rainier III, like many other monarchs, is also buried here. It was here too, that the wedding ceremony between Rainier III and Grace Kelly was conducted. The cathedral aside these events, is also considered remarkable for its architecture. Built in the year 1875, it is a magnificent example of neo-Romanesque style. Saint Paul's Anglican Church Monaco is another beautiful neo-Romanesque building, built in the year 1925 by the bishop of Gibraltar.

Any tourist will definitely find walking around the Champions Promenade a pleasure, and especially for those who are keen about football. Here, just like Hollywood's "Walk of Fame", there are prints of the hands and feet of famous football players. In general, Monte Carlo is a kind of Hollywood for football players and football fans; here everyone will be reminded of this. Staying here on a visit, you can accidentally stumble on the players celebrating the victory (or loss) of a match in any establishment.

It is definitely taking a walk along the port of Monte Carlo. As a matter of fact, the city seems to open up its "soul" right about here. Stylish yachts, attention-grabbing sculptures, crystal clear water, and the famous Monte Carlo rally (if your visit should coincide with it), will make you wish to stay here forever. In the evening, concerts are often held here. Also in the city there are other interesting museums, except the Museum of Cousteau. We are referring to the Collection de Voitures Anciennes de S.A.S. le Prince de Monaco, which houses the most sophisticated cars of Prince Rainier III, as well as the Musée des Timbres et des Monnaies, which attracts all philatelists, and the Musee Naval de Monaco, where you can see interesting models of ships

Monte Carlo Attractions and Nightlife

City break in Monte Carlo. Active leisure ideas for Monte Carlo - attractions, recreation and nightlife

Perhaps, the legendary Casino of Monte Carlo remains the main entertainment center of the city. However, in addition to the grand gambling facility there are many other attractive places which are recommended for visiting by fans of active pastime. The majority of famous discos and nightclubs are located near Spelugies quarter. As there are really many institutions here, each of them tries to attract customers by offering original cultural programs and other entertainments. "At Jimmy's" is very popular disco, which is located just a couple of steps away from the coast. Nearby you will find a popular sports club.

Among the theatres of the city we simply cannot fail to mention summer theater, which is located near the Larvotto peninsula, as well as Le Sporting cinema located next to the casino. Here you can always see newest movies and enjoy the comfort of a modern cinema. Those, who like a variety show, should not forget to visit Hall of Stars, where they will become the spectaculars of enchanting shows. Monte Carlo is one of the most attractive places for beach lovers. A diving club named Cap Dail is a popular place where you can rent all necessary equipment and even have training with an experienced instructor. Monaco Larvotto is a popular beach, near which are opened numerous restaurants and cafes. This place will be liked by fans of interesting and relaxing rest, and by those tourists, who cannot imagine a beach without funny sports entertainments. A ride on a yacht along the coast will bring you a great pleasure and will become an unforgettable evening entertainment.

There is a famous spa complex in Monte Carlo, which offers to its visitors a wide range of services. We are talking about Monte-Carlo Sporting Club. In addition to a huge number of treatments and recreational activities the club offers to its guests a variety of sports. Here you will find a large artificial beach and swimming pools with water attractions and slides. Monte-Carlo Sporting Club is a great destination for the whole family.

In Monaco, as well as in other European countries, you will be able to find services for bike renting. But why do you need a bike, when you can walk all the city in less than 2 hours. In Monaco, you can walk well: the Old Town, the Princely Palace, the casino and the Monte Carlo Opera, Fort Antoine, the Road of Sculptures. From the Principality, you can go to the French Riviera of France or to Italy. An alternative to pedestrian walks - special tourist trains Azur Express, which cover the main attractions. They can be found on the parking, on Saint-Martin avenue. A half-hour excursion is accompanied by comments in French, English, Italian, and German.

If you are looking for some exciting and active activities, here you will find all of them like windsurfing, diving, water skiing, wakeboarding, water scooters, yachting, jet-skiing, tennis, golf, cycling. In Monaco, green oases are cultivated and residents are deservedly proud of numerous gardens and parks. It is worth to visit the Japanese Garden, the Exotic Garden, the grotto of the observatory, the rosaries, the gardens of Saint-Martin. With children, you can go to the zoo. You can also go on a sea safari, make a walk by helicopter, the boat trip along the Gulf of Monaco

Monte Carlo Travel Tips

Preparing your trip to Monte Carlo: advices & hints - things to do and to obey

1. Tourists are better not to travel in autumn. It's raining heavily on this time of a year, so weather can disrupt the excursion seriously.

2. The majority of tourists visit the resort during the period from April to September, so if you plan to come here on this period, you should take care of bookings beforehand.

3. Travelers are advised to avoid drinking tap water. It is not dangerous for health, but it may negatively affect your well-being during the period of acclimatization.

4. Tips in the local restaurants are usually 10 - 15% of the total bill. As a rule, in large establishments tips are automatically included in the bill.

5. Fans of shopping should visit such designer shops as Hermes, Dior, Chanel and Cartier. The

embankment area is the best place for buying souvenirs as the majority of souvenir shops are located there.

6. Casinos of Monte Carlo are simply stunning, so not only fans of gaming, but also art lovers are recommended to visit them. Its halls are decorated with beautiful frescoes and sculptures, which are certainly worth to be seen by all guests of the city.

7. Only persons aged 21 years and older can attend casinos. Young people should take a passport in order to avoid misunderstandings.

8. When you plan your travel to Monte Carlo, do not forget to take a phrase book with you. The locals are very friendly to visitors, who try to communicate using their native language.

9. Shopping fans should visit «degriffes» shops. They sell branded clothing of past seasons, which has not been sold-out in major shopping

complexes. Despite the fact that the products sold here usually do not match latest fashion trends, the quality of clothes deserves the highest praise.

10. While going to a prestigious restaurant, you should choose the right outfit. Sloppily or too informally dressed visitors may be considered rude and uneducated

Monte Carlo Top Hotels

Best hotels for short vacation or business trip to Monte Carlo

Hôtel de Paris

From Monte Carlo center - 1.1 km

Small Monte Carlo is incredibly rich in high-class hotels. Hôtel de Paris has always been one of the most famous hotels in the city. The luxury hotel is open in a beautiful building that dates back to 1864. Besides posh guest rooms, clients of the hotel get exclusive access to Thermes Marins Monte-Carlo Spa. Gourmet travelers are, certainly, aware of Louis XV-Alain Ducasse restaurant that was awarded three Michelin stars. The restaurant serves delicious Mediterranean cuisine. There is an American-style bar at the hotel that regularly has live music and hosts various shows. It is hard to find a better destination for the evening. Finally, travelers are welcome to visit the old wine cellar and sample best sorts of vintage wine.

Hôtel Hermitage
From Monte Carlo center - 0.9 km
When it comes to describing historical hotels in Monte Carlo, it would be a mistake to forget to mention Hôtel Hermitage. This hotel is open in an eye-catching building in Renaissance style, and 6,600 square-meter large spa center is one of the main amenities available. Guest rooms look incredibly posh and are made in different styles and color combinations. Absolutely all rooms have panoramic floor-to-ceiling windows and beautiful

antique furniture. In some rooms, the design looks very cute because of numerous stuffed toys. Guests can leave their rooms are relax in the interior garden whenever they want. Finally, don't forget about Limùn Bar that serves fresh baking.

Le Méridien Beach Plaza
From Monte Carlo center - 2.3 km
Of course, there are prestigious resort hotels in Monte Carlo, and Le Méridien Beach Plaza is one of them. Only a few steps separate the hotel from the coastline. Le Méridien Beach Plaza has a private beach and a comfortable adjusting territory. Awesome beaches with panoramic views, terraces surrounded with exotic plants and a great choice of entertainments travelers can easily find an interesting and exciting pastime to fit their taste at this hotel. Nearly every day, interesting events and performances take place in L'intempo

restaurant. Female travelers will enjoy their visit to the hotel's beauty salon.

Metropole Monte-Carlo
From Monte Carlo center - 1.2 km
One of the most prominent designer hotels in Monte Carlo, Metropole Monte-Carlo is a must-visit place. The design of the hotel's adjusting territory was developed by Karl Lagerfeld. The historical building of the hotel is surrounded by a beautiful landscape garden with charming terraces scattered among exotic plants and flower beds. The design of guest rooms is truly aristocratic and includes premium wooden furniture and draping made of elite textiles. Elegant retro style furniture pieces create a truly inimitable atmosphere.

Monte-Carlo Bay Hotel & Resort
Monte-Carlo Bay Hotel & Resort will easily fit different categories of travelers. The hotel is open in a beautiful building in the colonial style, which is

located just a few steps away from the seaside and is surrounded by a picturesque garden. The giant swimming pool with a lagoon, artificial waterfalls, and sandy bottom remains the main decoration of the adjusting territory. Monte Carlo Bay Hotel is surrounded by spacious terraces with landscape decorations. There are comfortable hydro-massage baths in the most secluded relaxation areas of the hotel.

Fans of unusual hotels are recommended to take a look at Maria Teresa Yacht. This hotel is open on a beautiful yacht and has only four comfortable rooms for its guests. The yacht is docked in Port Hercule, so there's nothing strange in the fact that the yacht is popular with fans of water sports. All guest rooms are well-equipped and have décor made of premium sorts of wood and natural fabrics. The deck of the unusual floating hotel is perfectly suitable for sunbathing and enjoying delicious cocktails and snacks. To the service of travelers, Maria Teresa Yacht offers a wide range of wellness treatments and a charming snack bar with a large menu.

Monte Carlo Shopping

Shopping in Monte Carlo authentic goods, best outlets, malls and boutiques

The popular spot with a very stylish name, Golden Circle remains the top destination for shopping. The area has formed around Casino Square and covers several nearby streets. Besides top gambling, the area is famous for its branded boutiques. Travelers, who value fashionable items by top couturier, will enjoy Golden Circle. Famous Dior and Gucci shops are open in the area as well. The price is high as expected, but that is fully compensated by high quality and exclusiveness of the goods available for sale.

If the choice of elite shops available in Golden Circle is not enough for you, it is high time to make a walk along Larvotto beach. The most famous designer shops are open close to the coastline. Here, visitors can shop ready clothes or order a tailor made piece. The price range is also not really affordable, so many travelers visit Larvotto shops not to buy something, but simply to walk and look at shiny display windows. The shops in this area offer not only trendy designer clothes but also premium accessories, for example, fancy female bags, the price of which can reach several thousand dollars.

In Monte Carlo, there are several large trading centers, and Galaxie de Metropole is known as one of the biggest and most expensive. The department store is home to more than 80 boutiques, many of which are also targeted at the upscale clientele. It is the right place to search a magnificent evening dress, an elegant designer suit or exclusive shoes and bags. There are also several awesome jewelry stores in the center.

Fontvieille Shopping Centre is distinguished by a lot more affordable price tag. As there are no outlets in Monte Carlo, Fontvieille Shopping Centre is the best shopping destination for savvy travelers. Inside the center, you will find boutiques and shops by famous European brands that are known for their democratic pricing. Fontvieille is also a great place to shop interesting souvenirs, sports clothes and accessories, inexpensive perfumes and items for the home. Sales happen every season, and during that period visitors can purchase various items at a significant discount.

Elite jewelry shops are another distinguishing feature of Monte Carlo, and Fred Boutique remains one of the best and most famous jewelry salons in the whole city. The shop is famous far beyond the borders of the city, so even members of royal families make purchases there. As it is not hard to guess, the prices are impressive, but all jewelry pieces are absolutely flawless and are made of precious materials and stones. Fred Boutique sells only the most outstanding designer jewelry and the most beautiful precious stones.

Female travelers, who are not ready to shed outrageously big money for new jewelry, are recommended to visit Bijoux Cassio that offers a wide choice of fashion jewelry. The jewelry sold in this shop is distinguished by high quality. Actually, some jewelry pieces are so skillfully made that only a professional goldsmith can say whether it is genuine fine jewelry with precious stones or an imitation. The prices are very affordable at Bijoux Cassio, so fashionistas can easily buy precise copies of some fine jewelry that is available in the most luxurious and expensive jewelry shops of Monte Carlo.

When it's time to buy souvenirs, guests of the city are recommended to visit Condamine market. Here, one can buy many interesting handmade items. Among the souvenirs available for sale, it's easy to find many premium items that would become a worthy addition to any home decor.

One more famous historical shop, Boutique du Rocher is a great place to search for memorable souvenirs of the highest quality. Princess Grace herself was the founder of this shop. The opening took place in the 60s of the previous century. Nowadays, this shop sells incredibly beautiful ceramics, amazing photo frames, and many other home decorations. The prices of the majority of the items sold at Boutique du Rocher are affordable. Moreover, during more than 50 years, all the money got from sales are donated to charity. Fans of exclusive items would be happy to know that all the items are hand-made.

Transportation

Monaco Taxis and Car Rental

Taxis are a safe and affordable way to get around Monaco. Rates are determined by zone and time of day. There is a flat fee to get to the airport in Nice which include baggage fees and tolls. Currently, there is only one 24-hour cab company that can be booked in advance, *Radio Taxi* (+377-8-20-20-98-98), but taxis can be flagged down on the street or picked up at designated stands.

Many visitors from Europe choose to drive to Monaco and during the summer months, this can lead to major traffic jams in the small principality. In the summer, it is estimated that 100,000 cars go in and out on any given day. Keeping this in mind, street parking is strictly enforced and visitors are advised to park in public lots instead. Car rentals are readily available either at the airport in Nice or in Monaco itself. Most international companies have offices, including Hertz, Avis and Europcar, but booking in advance is a must during the peak summer months.

Monaco Water Taxis

There is a so-called electric boat bus in Monaco. The water taxi provides service every day from Quai Kennedy to Terre-plein du Fort Antoine (on either side of Port Hercules) from 8:00 a.m. to 7:50 p.m. Visitors can buy a single trip ticket, 10-ride pass or Daily Tourist Card, which allows unlimited use of the buses and water taxis.

Monaco Trains and Buses

Monaco has an excellent public transportation system and visitors are encouraged to purchase the Daily Tourist Card, which allows for unlimited use of the buses and water taxis.

There are five bus routes operated by the Compagnie des Autobus de Monaco. Buses generally come every 10 minutes Monday through Friday and every 20 minutes on weekends until 9:30 p.m. daily. A less frequent night bus is available until just past midnight.

There is no rail network within Monaco; however, the principality is well-connected to the French train system. From Monaco, visitors can take the TGV to Paris, as well as other connections to Milan, Genoa, Basel, Strasbourg, Toulouse, Pisa, and Rome. There is also a Regional Express Train (TER), which provides links to other cities on the French Riviera.

Airports

Nice Cote d'Azur Airport

Monaco does not have its own airport so the closest place to fly from is Nice Cote d'Azur Airport, the third busiest airport in France. The facility is located along the coast, about thirty minutes southwest by car. It is also possible to reach the airport by helicopter, using the Heli Air Monaco service. The flying time is just seven minutes and there are about 70 flights a day from Monaco to the airport.

The airport handles just over nine million passengers a year and has two terminals, which are connected via a free shuttle bus. Over 30 airlines fly in and out of Nice Cote d'Azur Airport, half as regularly scheduled flights and half as seasonal or charters. The airport has both domestic and international connections. The most popular international destinations are Rome, Vienna, Moscow, London, Amsterdam, and Munich. Delta Air Lines offers seasonal flights to New York-JFK.

There are plenty of restaurants, cafés and bars in both terminals and a range of newsagents, souvenir shops and duty-free stores for international travelers. Other facilities include a pharmacy, medical center and business center. Transportation from the airport to Monaco includes helicopter, bus or self-drive. There are plenty of car rental options at the airport, including Sixt and Europcar. The public bus from the airport to Monaco takes roughly one hour.

Visas and Vaccinations

Monaco is part of the Schengen Agreement and visitors who need a visa to enter the EU will only need one at their first entry point into the

European Union states (if that is not Monaco or France). US and Canadian citizens do not need a visa to enter Monaco for stays up to 90 days. Up to date requirements can be viewed from the French Embassy in Washington DC (http://ambafrance-us.org/spip.php?rubrique=2). If you are arriving overland from France, there are no formal entry requirements.

Health and Safety

There are no vaccinations required for travel to Monaco and no specific health risks. Monaco is generally safe and the police are serious about keeping tourists and the many VIPs that visit the principality protected. The only threat is potentially petty theft. Travelers should keep their valuables in their hotel safe and generally be aware of their surroundings, especially at night. The area around the train station is seen as the highest risk for pickpockets. Never leave anything of value in your car and make sure to lock the doors when parked

Weather

Monaco enjoys a beautiful Mediterranean climate thanks to its ideal location in the South of France. This means that summers are dry and warm with mild, slightly rainy winters. Temperatures during the peak summer months range from 69°F to 78°F, with very little precipitation. In winter, the temperatures drop to between 48°F to 56°F.

The principality sees the largest amount of rain during October and November, but this should not deter visitors. In fact, those willing to risk it will find lower hotel rates and no lines at the popular restaurants.

Best Time to Visit Monaco

Summer is undoubtably Monaco's busiest and warmest season when the European and international glitterati flock to the beachfront shores. Many of the popular arts and music festivals take place during this time, catering to the high-end vacationers. Hotels tend to fill up and popular restaurants will require advance booking. This is also the most expensive time to visit Monaco.

To avoid the crowds and save some money, coming in the spring or fall can be a nice option. The weather is not as hot as in the summer, but is still pleasant. However, big events during the off-season also attract big crowds, so unless you're coming specifically for the Formula 1 Grand Prix or the Monte-Carlo Rolex Masters it does make sense to avoid these dates.

Monaco Holidays and Festivals

For a small city state, there are a surprising number of internationally renowned Monaco holidays and events. Partially attracted by the prestige and money in the principality, artists and athletes from all over the world come to Monaco for festivals and fun in the sun. Grace Kelly, the former Princess of Monaco, was a famous American actress prior to marrying Prince Rainier, and she put a lot of effort into developing the fine arts scene and inspiring Hollywood intrigue.

International Circus Festival
Started in 1974 by Prince Rainier, he personally loved circuses and wanted to create a venue where everyone could enjoy a world class show. Since then, circus acts from all over the world come to Monaco in January to perform. Judged on technical difficulty and creativity, the best

performances receive the Gold and Silver Clown Awards.

Rose Ball

One of the most elegant and coveted fundraising events of the year is the Rose Ball, held annually in March. Started in 1954 by Grace Kelly, all proceeds goes to the Princess Grace Foundation. Each year the ball has a different theme and is known for the thousands of roses that are used to decorate the Salle des Etoiles venue.

Spring Arts Festival

Monaco's annual Spring Arts Festival in April attracts artists from all around world. The festival showcases music, dance, arts, and theatre performances held in world-class venues throughout the principality. This is a popular event so tickets need to be purchased well in advance.

Formula 1 Monaco Grand Prix

Racing enthusiasts should not miss the opportunity to see Formula 1 cars whizzing through the streets of Monaco. The Monaco Grand Prix, taking place in May each year, is one of the few street racing circuits on the Formula 1 calendar and not much has changed since it's inception in 1955.

Concerts at the Prince's Palace
Outdoor concerts take place at the palace throughout the summer which were started by Prince Rainier III. Open to the public, visitors are encouraged to purchase tickets in advance to avoid disappointment. The venue is simply breathtaking and the Monte-Carlo Philharmonic Orchestra usually has a beautiful line-up of shows. Concerts begin at 9:30 p.m. and visitors are expected to be seated on time.

Monte-Carlo International Fireworks Festival
Considered one of the best fireworks festivals in the world, this late summer event has been taking

place since 1966. Scheduled in July or August, the fireworks are shot from Fort Antoine over the water by pyrotechnics from all over the world competing to put on the best show.

Monaco Yacht Show
Sailing enthusiasts should not miss the annual Monaco Yacht Show in September. Over 100 of the most beautiful and impressive yachts are on display at Port Hercules and 500 vendors come to showcase their wares, a sailing enthusiast's dream.

Monaco International Marathon
Although this marathon is not on the major running curcuit, it is the only marathon in the world that traverses three countries: France, Italy and Monaco. Between 1,000 and 2,000 people participate in this marathon annually in November.

Monaco Activities
Casino

Casinos have been shaping Monaco and making it legendary since 1863. Today, Monaco remains the finest and most luxurious destination of all for high rollers and the general public alike, because its casinos are constantly reinventing themselves. Preserving tradition yet always innovating.

The ultimate way to discover Monaco. It all begins at the legendary Place du Casino, the vibrant, glamorous beating heart of the Principality. The square is home to the Casino de Monte-Carlo - the epitome of luxury.

The slot-machine paradise of the Casino Café de Paris, renowned for its innovation, is merely steps away. The nearby Sun Casino is Monaco's "Little Vegas", while the Monte-Carlo Bay Casino sits inside an exclusive Resort.

Gaming, and so much more. Monaco has sustained its appeal because it has been reinventing itself since the end of the 19th century. Visitors from all over the world are drawn to the lively Principality for its extensive range of fun activities.

The casinos of the Société des Bains de Mer are no exception, each one offering much more than casino games or slot machines. With their lounge areas, gourmet restaurants and pop-up art installations, they are all places to see and be seen in Monaco.

Casino de Monte-Carlo

Open to games every day from 2 pm.
Open for visits in the morning from 10 am to 1 pm*

François Blanc, the casino's founder once said, "we should do nothing here as it is done elsewhere". The image of James Bond has become inseparable from the Casino de Monte-Carlo, which, with its

Belle Époque architecture, is a reference for gaming and entertainment, not just in Europe but around the world.

An exceptional selection. French Roulette, Trente et Quarante, Baccarat, Black Jack and Poker Texas Hold'em Ultimate. New and occasional players try their luck at the table games under the warm glow of Bohemian crystal chandeliers, while slot machine players hunt down lady luck in the Salle Renaissance or Salle des Amériques.

Unique savoir-faire. Everything here is about sophistication and attention to detail, to create an immersive experience in the casino world. The gaming tables are crafted by artisans in the Société des Bains de Mer's own workshops and the croupiers ensure players receive world-class service and benefit from their unrivalled know-how.

Gaming, and so much more - from seasoned players to newcomers, there is something here for everyone: entertainment, thrills, unforgettable emotions and surprises!

Casino Café de Paris

Open 24 hours a day, 7 days a week.
The Casino Café de Paris is famous for its 480 state-of-the-art slot machines. It also offers table games and electronic games, for an electric atmosphere inside the resort's most innovative establishment. This generous and vibrant casino is open 24/7.

Slot machine paradise. The Casino Café de Paris never sleeps and offers players the greatest selection of slot machines, some of which are found nowhere else in the world. Not forgetting the table games: Blackjack, Punto Banco, French roulette, American roulette and Ultimate Texas

Hold'em, where aficionados can try their luck. The Casino Café de Paris is an irresistible playground for adrenaline-seekers.

An experience powered by innovation. Along with its incredible array of slot machines, the Casino Café de Paris has gaming tables indoors and on its two smoking terraces, the ideal way to try your luck while enjoying a drink and admiring the Casino's gardens. The hospitality is always friendly and impeccable. Earlybird players will find breakfast served daily, with tea time and welcome cocktails served later in the day.

A generous casino. The jackpots here are the highest on the French Riviera, sometimes up to a million. With its contemporary décor, the Casino Café de Paris is where casual and seasoned players can enjoy the full casino experience, Monte-Carlo style!

Sun Casino

Open every day from 2 pm.
The highly contemporary Sun Casino is a glittering establishment just a stone's throw from the Place du Casino. It is the Principality's Las Vegas, a chic, welcoming venue full of contrasts and offering American-style entertainment.

American-style party atmosphere. Just a few steps from the Place du Casino, the Sun Casino can be accessed via the Fairmont Monte Carlo lobby and from the famous Spélugues hairpin curve. Inside, time stands still as players are welcomed by warm and vibrant colours that plunges them immediately into the ambiance of this newly renovated casino.

One floor, many atmospheres. At the Sun Casino, the atmosphere is resolutely friendly and ultra-modern, while still offering certain cosier areas that are just as festive, such as the Sun Lounge bar that shows regulary live music, DJ sets and sporting events. Players will be delighted with the selection of table games, slots and electronic games.

Introduction to casino games. The Sun Casino welcomes groups and offers an introductory blackjack lesson. This is a chance to try English Roulette, Black Jack, Punto Banco, Three Card Poker, 3Card Poker and Texas Hold'em Poker in a prestige setting, and why not come back later, alone or with friends!

Museum

Monaco's Oceanographic Museum

An unwanted visitor from Australia lurks inside the Oceanographic Museum in Monaco. White-spotted jellyfish hitched a lift from Queensland to the Mediterranean in ship's ballast in the 1960s and have since been doing rather well in their new environment. Their descendants float about, stinging unsuspecting swimmers off Spanish beaches and threatening native shrimp.

The white-spotted jellyfish in the museum's aquarium is rather beautiful though, resembling a placid, floating pincushion of vivid white dots. It has the trailing, feathery skirts of a can-can dancer. Not so attractive is the jellyfish's sex life. Males release sperm in the water and females gather it into their mouths, where they hold eggs until they hatch.

If you want to be alternatively enchanted and revolted, then Monaco's Oceanographic Museum is the place to be. It's the principality's unexpected treat, at once a serious scientific research centre, an entertainment and an education. Founder Prince Albert I was a scientist and oceanographer, and Jacques Cousteau was once director. It has cutting-edge displays, yet parts are endearingly old fashioned, hearkening back to the days when Edwardian-era aristocrats had unlimited budgets and a liking for the weird and wonderful.

The 1910 neoclassical museum building is Monaco's most prominent structure. Many mistake it for the palace. It looms on a clifftop like the mad retreat of a James Bond villain, with a facade encrusted with motifs of crabs and scorpionfish and octopus. Its main hall is a magnificent cabinet of curiosities from another era. You can clamber into a 1776 Bushnell Tortoise submarine, which resembles a giant wine barrel with a screw cap. There are strange diving suits, a stuffed polar bear, sea fossils, ship models and marble busts.

In the Whale Room, gigantic skeletons dangle from the ceiling. They look like dinosaurs and have open jaws of serrated teeth. The narwhal brandishes a javelin-like horn. Touch screens below tell you more, and an hourly sound-and-light show entrances kids.

There are some 6000 live specimens, too. This is one of the world's oldest aquariums. A moray eel acquired in 1969 is still alive and well, and some sharks and other fish are 40 years old. There have been tropical tanks here since the 1930s, and Monaco was among the pioneers of the delicate task of keeping notoriously temperamental coral in artificial environments.

Its centrepiece is a 450,000-litre tank holding an entire coral ecosystem. Some of its corals are now 20 years old, a first in the history of aquariums. The most stunning display is a pool of fluorescent coral, including luminous purple and pink Montiposa, waving green Galaxea and lurid Blastomusa that look like 1970s lava lamps.

The Shark Lagoon is rather grey in comparison, but its creatures are splendid. There are several types of shark, rays, a rather lonely hawksbill turtle and an outsized guitarfish that looks like a stealth bomber from the distant future. The kids can touch a baby shark and shark's eggs at the touch tank, as well as crabs and starfish. If you've never seen a shark's egg before, you'll be astonished.

Don't leave without heading roof-wards for glorious views over Monaco and the French Riviera. Below on the rocks, pygmy cormorants breed. Squint out to sea and you might see one of the slender fin whales that live off the coast. There may be 800 of them, but no one is quite sure. We don't know much at all about our oceans and seas. To its great credit, the Oceanographic Museum makes you think what a shame that is, because even its own modest show of marine life is a marvel.

Quick Guide to Monaco for New Travlers

To Get in

Although not a member of either the European Union or the European Economic Area, Monaco maintains an open border and customs union with France and is treated as part of the Schengen Area. Both French and Monégasque authorities carry out checks at Monaco's seaport and heliport.

A souvenir passport stamp may be obtained at the national tourist office. This is located at 2a Boulevard des Moulins, which is north of the garden across from the Casino. Weekend hours are short.

By plane

The nearest airport is the Nice Côte-d'Azur International, which is around 40 kilometres (24 miles) away from the city-centre in neighbouring

France. It operates daily flights from nearly all of Europe's main cities, such as London and Paris. There are regular Rapide Cote D'Azur buses connecting Monte Carlo with both the terminals at Nice Côte-d'Azur airport, and taxis are always available outside the terminal buildings - although make sure a fee is agreed in advance or the meter is indeed switched on at the start of the journey, as shady French taxi drivers are notorious for charging tourists whatever they see fit.

By helicopter

Monacair is the sole operator of regular helicopter transfers between Nice Airport and the Monaco Heliport. After collecting your luggage at the Nice airport, present yourself at the Monacair reception desks (in terminals 1 and 2). A ground crew will carry your luggage and drive you to the heliport. The flight along the coast is beautiful and only lasts 7 minutes. When arriving right at the Monaco heliport along the water's edge, a chauffeur will take you directly to your hotel. When leaving Monaco, a partnership with more than 40 airlines allows for a direct transfer to the boarding gate with your cabin luggage. Rates are €140 for one-way transfers, and €260 for round trips.

By train

The Monaco-Monte Carlo the boss station is very large, modern and mostly underground. There is an exit adjacent to platform C that, while not visible on Google Maps, is a five minute walk to the port. During the day tourist officials are typically available to help foreign travelers. It has good service to most of neighboring France and Italy. There are 2-4 services per hour to Nice, Cannes, Menton and Ventimiglia (Italy). Most international trains will stop, such as the 'Ligure' which links Marseilles and Milan, the 'train bleu' which operates between Paris and Ventimiglia, and the famous high-speed TGV which runs between Nice and Paris . A TGV train between Paris and Monte Carlo takes around 6 and a half hours. Be aware that there's no left-luggage in the train station nor in the rest of Monaco. There's a law in Monaco forbidding leaving bags etc. in any place.

If you are planning to visit Monte Carlo from Ventimiglia, don't wait for a ticket in the Trenitalia counters or auto-machines. Go straight to the travel agency (the only one) inside the station, which is marked with the sign of SNCF (French Railways). If you plan to come back buy your return also (€5.40 with return), ticket is open and you can validate it in auto machines without hour commitment of a particular train. Trains to and from Monte Carlo run every 15 minutes until late at night. The line is serviced by SNCF Regional Trains, which is the railway provider of Monaco.

The closest major airport is in Nice and, while the airport does not have a train station, the Nice-St. Augustin terminal is a 15 minute walk. The ticket is a flat €4.80 and is roughly 40 minutes. There are multiple trains per hour all day. The train travels more inland and through more tunnels and the bus - there are less coastal views - but is much easier from the airport.

For further information like price and times visit Trenitalia

The train ticket machines only accept credit cards that have computer chips (no magnetic stripe reader) or coins, and the ticket desk can be slow. So if your credit card does not have a computer chip, you can save time by bringing Euro coins with you.

By car

Monaco is accessed by its land borders from France or Italy by a network of highways, most commonly used of which is the A8 which runs west from Monte Carlo to Nice and Marseille, and east towards the Italian border. Make sure to take into account frequent traffic jams when approaching and leaving Monaco.

Between Nice and Monaco, there are also three more scenic roads: the Basse Corniche (Low Coast-Road - Highway 98), along the sea, the Moyenne Corniche (Middle Coast Road - Highway 7), going through Eze-Village, and the Grande Corniche (Great Coast Road), going through La Turbie and Col d'Eze (Eze Pass). All are pretty drives offering spectacular views over the Coast line. For an extra-special treat, rent a convertible sports car from the many airport rental services and take in the French Riviera in style.

Taxi trips to and from Nice cost around €80.

You can also use a private driver service for your displacements in Monaco Car with driver.

By bus

There is no bus station in Monte Carlo. Instead, international buses stop at various points throughout the city. Regular buses, run by Rapide Cote D'Azur, connects Monte Carlo with Nice and other French destinations. Services run regularly to many major French towns and cities. Route 100 leaves every 15 min from the port (Le Port) in Nice and costs €1.50. The bus trip offers fantastic views of the coast, but can get extremely crowded during peak hours.

An express shuttle, route 110, links the Nice Côte d'Azur Airport and the principality. A bus leaves every half hour and a single ticket costs €22 (May

2017). The bus stops near all major hotels throughout Monaco, not just Monte Carlo.

By boat

Monaco's two ports are no strangers to private yachts. Port Hercule is exceptionally beautiful and offers mooring and anchoring possibilities for up to five hundred vessels, some of which are extremely large and elegant (in fact, many tourists often take time out of their day to simply have a drink by the water and admire the fantastic super yachts). The Port of Fontvieille, integrated into the new district, can receive as many as 60 vessels of at least 30 meters in length. Both are large and well-equipped.

Monaco also serves as an embarkation port and port-of-call for cruises, so cruise ships can often be spotted using Port Hercule. It's breakwater offers a large pier able to support one large cruise ship. If in use, other ships must moor/anchor offshore, where tenders shuttle passengers to/from shore to either port...with preference for Port Hercule which offers substantially better walking distances than Fontvieille to the more popular sites.

At close proximity, the Port of Cap d'Ail is also a choice destination for pleasure-boats.

- ✓ Luxury Yacht Charter France offers a wide range of Luxury Mega Yachts for charter from Monaco
- ✓ Luxury Yacht Charter Monaco are experts for private Luxury Yachts on French riviera

To Get around

By foot

Walking is by far the best way to get around Monaco; however, there are some areas, such as the Exotic Gardens, that require a large change in elevation and therefore make for rather strenuous hikes. There are also seven public escalators and elevators (all free) that help negotiate the steep slopes of the city. If you find yourself afoot and wanting to reach the opposite bank of Port Hercule, look for the small pedestrian-only ferry that runs each 20 minutes or so during daylight; it costs only one Euro.

By bus

Monaco has an urban bus service, operated by the Compagnie des Autobus Monaco , which comprises of five bus routes (labeled 1, 2, 4, 5 and 6) serving 143 stops. Each stop has the bus number(s) that stop there, and most stops feature a real-time display showing waiting times for the next service. Each stop has a name and a network map. The service usually starts at around 0600 and runs right through until about 2100. Tickets can be purchased on board the buses themselves (€2), at many news vendors and shops throughout the city and at auto ticket machines in the stops (€1.50) - often it will be advertised as to where you can do this. A 24 hour pass can also be purchased from ticket machines or onboard the bus (€5.50). A night bus service operates in a circular route from 22.00 until 04.00.

By motor scooter

You can easily rent a motor scooter in Nice and take a short trip east along the sea into Monaco. The views are beautiful and the ride is fun along the twisty seaside road. There are plenty of places to park for free. Theft is not a concern, as there are cameras throughout and police everywhere. To rent one whilst there, you must be 16.

By bicycle

It is possible to hire a bicycle from the Auto-Moto-Garage on the Rue de Millo.

By car

Private cars are singularly useless for getting around Monaco, as you'll spend more time trying to park than if you walked or took a taxi instead.

International car hire companies do have offices at the airport in Nice and also in Monte Carlo city. These include Avis, Gare Monte Carlo, Europcar and Hertz - drivers must have held a national driving license for at least one year and it is usually requested that the cost is paid for with the driver's credit card. Driving in the city center can be intimidating in Monte Carlo with heavy traffic - however, it is often worth this to drive alongside the more expensive vehicles in the city! Make sure to request a car with an automatic gearbox if you are not used to driving manual.

By taxi

Taxis cannot be hailed on the streets (they won't stop) and there are two main taxi stands open around the clock at the Avenue de Monte Carlo and the railway station, although it is always best to agree a fee beforehand or make sure the meter is running. Most hotels will provide taxis or courtesy drivers. The best is to get the taxi service phone number to be able to call a taxi wherever your are.

Language

There are 125 different nationalities that reside in Monaco, hence many languages are spoken. French is the sole official language, however Monégasque is the national language. Italian and English are widely understood and spoken.

To See

The principality of Monaco offers a great balance of historical and modern attractions. There are various museums and palaces to visit as well as shopping malls and casinos. Monaco also offers relaxation spots along the harbor and even around the attractions. It is relatively easy to navigate Monte Carlo and Monaco if you take the time to learn where the various "short cuts" are. City maps are generally available at most news vendor stands and shops for a small fee.

Take a walk through Monaco-Ville, also known as "le rocher" or "the rock." Monaco-Ville is still a medieval village at heart and an astonishingly picturesque site. It is made up almost entirely of pedestrian streets and passageways and most previous century houses still remain. There a number of hotels, restaurant and souvenir shops tourists can stay, eat and shop at. You can also visit the Prince's Palace, the Cathedral, the

Oceanographic Museum, the City Hall, and the Saint Martin Gardens.

The Palais Princier (Prince's Palace) is in old Monaco-Ville and is worth a visit. There are audio-guided tours of the palace each day and usually run around the clock. The Palace also offers a breathtaking panoramic view overlooking the Port and Monte-Carlo. Everyday at 11:55 AM, in front of the Palace's main entrance visitors can watch the changing of the guard ceremony performed by the "Carabiniers." "Carabiniers" are not only in charge of the Prince's security but they offer Him a Guard of Honor and on special occasions, are His escorts. The "Compagnie des Carabiniers du Prince" has a military band (Fanfare); which performs at public concerts, official occasions, sports events and international military music festivals.

The Monaco Cathedral was built in 1875 and stands on the site of a 13th century earlier church. It is a mock Romanesque-Byzantine church dedicated to Saint Nicolas and houses the remains of former Princes of Monaco and Princess Grace. The church square also contains some of Monaco-Ville's finest restaurants.

The Oceanographic Museum and Aquarium is a world-renowned attraction. Located 279 above sea level, the museum contains stunning collections of marine fauna, numerous specimens of sea creatures (stuffed or in skeleton form), models of Prince Albert's laboratory ships, and craft ware made from the sea's natural products. On the ground floor, exhibitions and film projections are presented daily in the Conference room. In the basement, visitors can take pleasure in watching spectacular shows of marine flora and fauna. With 4,000 species of fish and over 200 families of invertebrates, the aquarium is now an authority on the presentation of the Mediterranean and tropical marine ecosystem. Lastly, visitors can have lunch in "La Terrasse" and visit the museum gift shop. The entrance fee is 16€ for adults. Students can get discount by showing valid student ID. You need to take bus number 1 or 2 from the Monaco Monte Carlo train station to reach this aquarium.

The Jardin Exotique (Exotic Gardens) is one of the many gardens Monaco has to offer. Several thousand rare plants from around the world are presented in a walking tour that is quite memorable for the views as well as the flora and plants. The collection is mostly cacti, so do not expect to see a broad variety. Due to the rise in altitude, not only are there many displays of desert plants but there are a handful of subtropical flora displays as well. There is also a grotto (cave) that has scheduled guided tours. The tour (in French only) starts at the beginning of every hour and lasts for around 25 minutes. In the cave, you will have to climb the stairs equivalent to around a 6 storied building. The entry cost is a bit steep (€8) unless you're under 16 or a student (€3.50). You need to take bus number 2 to reach this Garden. You can take this bus either from the train station or from the Oceanographic Museum.

The Church of the Sacred Heart (Eglise du Sacré-Coeur) or Church of the Moneghetti, not far from the Jardin Exotique, stands out as as one of the most representative art déco churches in Monaco. Built by the Italian Jesuit fathers from 1926 to 1929 as a sanctuary for prayer and adoration, its remarkable frescoes by Italian painter Franzoni revealed their original bright colors in the renovation works completed in 2015.

La Condamine is the second oldest district in Monaco, after Monaco-Ville. Here you can stop and marvel at the many luxurious yachts and cruise ships which usually adorn the docks in the marina. La Condamine is a thriving business district where you can visit the Condamine Market and rue Princesse-Caroline mall. With enjoyable landscaped areas and modern buildings, La Condamine is surely worth a visit.

The Monaco Opera House or Salle Garnier was built by the famous architect Charles Garnier. The auditorium of the opera house is decorated in red and gold and has frescoes and sculptures all around the auditorium. Looking up to the ceiling of the auditorium, the visitor will be blown away by the superb paintings. The opera house is flamboyant but at the same time very beautiful. There have been some of the most superior international performances of ballet, opera and concerts held in the opera house for more than a century; consider taking in a show during your visit... but expect to pay top dollar!

The Marlborough Fine Arts Gallery was founded in London by Frank Lloyd and Harry Fischer. A second gallery was opened in Rome, another in New York, and one more in Monaco. The gallery holds a grand collection of post-World War II artists and even paintings by Pablo Picasso, Joan Miró, Jules Brassai, Louise Bourgeois, Dale Chihuly, David Hockney and Henri Matisse. Admission is free and the gallery also offers group exhibitions.

The Grimaldi Forum is the Monaco convention center. Completed in July 2000, the sun filled building on the sea has a remarkable glass entrance, two convention restaurants, an auditorium for ballet and opera, and two more auditoriums for meetings and other affairs. The

Forum also offers two large exhibition halls that can be used for trade shows or other exhibitions. It is also a short walking distance from surrounding hotels.

The Prince's car collection For any car enthusiast, it is the place to go, there is everything, from carriges and old cars, to formula 1 race cars.

To Do

If your wallet permits it, try your luck in the Grand Casino and gamble alongside the world's richest and often most famous. You'll need your passport to enter (as Monégasque citizens are prohibited from gambling at the casino), and the fees for entry range enormously depending on what room you are going to - often from €30 right up into the hundreds. You can also visit the casino without gambling, but also for a nominal fee. The dress code inside is extremely strict - men are required to wear coats and ties, and casual or tennis shoes are forbidden. The gaming rooms themselves are spectacular, with stained glass, paintings, and sculptures everywhere. There are two other more Americanized casinos in Monte Carlo. Neither of these has an admission fee, and the dress code is more casual.

Scenic flights: enjoy Monaco and the surrounding French Riviera from above with a scenic helicopter tour. Monacair offers flights starting from €65 per passenger on a 6 passengers flight. Their helicopters with air-conditioning and open-cabin design allow for a 180° sweeping view to admire the breathtaking view over the Principality. Tours can be booked online or at the Monacair reception desk at Monaco Heliport.

Monaco's streets hosts the best known Formula 1 Grand Prix. It is also one of Europe's premier social highlights of the year. The Automobile Club of Monaco organizes this spectacular Formula 1 race each year. The Grand Prix is 78 laps around 3.34 kilometers of Monte Carlo's most narrow and twisted streets. The main attraction of the Monaco Grand Prix is the proximity of the speeding Formula One cars to the race spectators. The thrill of screaming engines, smoking tires and determined drivers also makes the Monaco Grand Prix one of the most exciting races in the world. There are more than 3,000 seats available for sale on the circuit ranging from €90 to more than €500. Monaco residents often rent out their terraces for the event with prices ranging from €8,000 to €140,000 for the four days. During the off season, it is possible to walk around the circuit. Tourist office maps have the route clearly marked on their maps, although devotees won't need them! For those who can afford it, you can also take a ride around the track in a performance car.

Aquavision: Discover Monaco from the sea during this fascinating boat tour! "Aquavision" is a catamaran-type boat equipped with two windows in the hull for underwater vision, thus allowing the passengers to explore the natural seabed of the coast in an unusual way. The boat can take up to 120 people per journey. The cost for adults is €11, while the cost for children and students ages 3-18 is €8.

Azur Express: Fun tourist trains make daily tours all over Monaco. You will visit the Monaco Port, Monte-Carlo and its Palaces, the famous Casino and its gardens, the Old Town for City Hall and finally the royal Prince's Palace. Commentaries are in English, Italian, German and French. This enjoyable tour runs about 30 minutes long and cost is €6; children under age 5 ride free.

In the summer time, Monte-Carlo is illuminated with dazzling concerts at the exclusive Monte-Carlo Sporting Club. The club has featured such artist as Natalie Cole, Andrea Bocelli, the Beach Boys, Lionel Richie and Julio Iglesias among others. The club also hosts a small casino which includes basic casino games. With no one under the age of 18, the rate per person is €20.

While staying in Monaco, you can take a full-day-journey (or half-day-journey, whichever you prefer) to surrounding areas like France and Italy. Monaco is connected to France by highways so renting a car would be the best way to go. You can also take the "train bleu" or a bus to European cities closer to Monaco including Paris, Nice and Ventimiglia. If you want to travel to farther countries in Europe, do so by plane. Amsterdam, Rome, London, Brussels, Frankfurt and Zurich are less than two hours away by plane.

Yacht charters in Monaco are very popular and there are several companies who can arrange a trip either on a small boat, a bareboat yacht or on a luxury superyacht.

Monaco and the surrounding areas are beautiful and the region and especially the Casino are famous for being a mecca for luxury cars, such as Ferraris, Lamborghinis and Bentleys. One very popular activity for visitors to Monaco is to rent a luxury car for a few hours or for a day to enjoy the stunning coastal roads.

Get a Monaco stamp in your passport at the tourist information center. It's free.

To Buy

Monaco has the euro (€) as its sole currency along with 24 other countries that use this common European money. These 24 countries are: Austria, Belgium, Cyprus, Estonia, Finland, France, Germany, Greece, Ireland, Italy, Latvia, Lithuania, Luxembourg, Malta, the Netherlands, Portugal, Slovakia, Slovenia and Spain (official euro members which are all European Union member states) as well as Andorra, Kosovo, Monaco, Montenegro, San Marinoand the Vatican which use it without having a say in eurozone affairs and without being European Union members. Together, these countries have a population of more than 330 million.

One euro is divided into 100 cents. While each official euro member (as well as Monaco, San Marino and Vatican) issues its own coins with a unique obverse, the reverse, as well as all bank notes, look the same throughout the eurozone.

Every coin is legal tender in any of the eurozone countries.

Shopping in Monte Carlo is usually quite exclusive and is certainly no place for a budget holiday. There are plenty of places to melt the credit card alongside Europe's high rollers. The chic clothes shops are in the Golden Circle, framed by Avenue Monte Carlo, Avenue des Beaux-Arts and Allees Lumieres, where Hermes, Christian Dior, Gucci and Prada all have a presence. The area on and around Place du Casino is home to high-end jewelers such as Bulgari, Cartier and Chopard. You will find, however, that most tourists will simply enjoy wandering the area and window shopping, even if you don't buy anything. The normal shopping hours are from 9AM to noon and 3PM to 7PM.

For a more cultured take on shopping in Monte Carlo, try the Condamine Market. The market, which can be found in the Place d'Armes, has been in existence since 1880 and is lively and attractive - many hours can be spent simply wandering around, bargaining for souvenirs from the many tiny shops, boutiques and friendly locals. If however, your shopping tastes are more modern, just take a short walk along the esplanade to the rue Princess Caroline pedestrian mall.

The Fontvieille Shopping Centre is also a more "normal" shopping experience with 36 shops selling electronic goods, CDs, furniture, and clothes as well as a Carrefour supermarket and McDonald's. The tourist office also issues a useful free shopping guide to the city.

Some stores to browse or buy:

Fred Boutique, 6, av des Beaux-Arts, Monte Carlo 98000. Located on the exclusive avenue of des Beaux-Arts, this is one of only a handful of Fred boutiques in the world. An official jeweler of Monaco's royal family and a favorite of celebrities, you may not be able to afford much in this boutique, but its worth a jaw dropping visit. If you go to Monte Carlo, you shouldn't miss this.

Boutique du Rocher, 1, av de la Madone, Monte Carlo 98000. Opened by Princess Grace in the 60's, travelers still flock here to grab the very best in take home souvenirs. Choose from hand-carved frames and mirrors, ceramics, homewares and toys. Prices are moderate and all proceeds go to local charities.

Davidoff, 17, av des Spélugues, Les galeries du Métropole, Monte Carlo 98000. High end cigar and cigarette store, where you are assisted by staff that know their product well.

Galerie Moghadam, 23 & 41, bd des Moulins, Monte Carlo 98000. Award-winning speciality shop that offers superb hand woven tapestries and carpets.

Pratoni Monaco, 7, Avenue Princesse Grace (Larvotto), 10-12 :30/14-19 :30. Monaco fashion brand Pratoni offers a variety of ready-to-wear clothing & accessories for gentlemen in addition to wide range of made-to-measure services. All items are of high quality and made in Italy or Monaco.

The End

Made in the USA
Las Vegas, NV
21 January 2022

41985588R00146